# fallen CHAINS

# fallen CHAINS

A Woman's Journey from Bondage to Freedom

## SAMANTHA OVERTON CAMPBELL

COOKE HOUSE
PUBLISHING
WINSTON SALEM

# FALLEN CHAINS: A WOMAN'S JOURNEY FROM BONDAGE TO FREEDOM

Copyright © 2016 – Samantha Campbell

All rights reserved. This book is protected by the copyright laws of the United States of America. This book may not be copied or reprinted for commercial gain or profit. The use of quotations or occasional page copying for personal or group study is permitted and encouraged. Permission will be granted upon request.

Unless otherwise identified, Scripture quotations are from the King James Version. Copyright © 1982 by Thomas Nelson, Inc. Used by permission. All rights reserved.

Scripture quotations marked (NIV) are taken from the Holy Bible, New International Version®, NIV®. Copyright © 1973, 1978, 1984, 2011 by Biblica, Inc.™ Used by permission of Zondervan. All rights reserved worldwide. www.zondervan.com The "NIV" and "New International Version" are trademarks registered in the United States Patent and Trademark Office by Biblica, Inc.™

Scripture quotations are taken from the Holy Bible, New Living Translation, copyright ©1996, 2004, 2007, 2013, 2015 by Tyndale House Foundation. Used by permission of Tyndale House Publishers, Inc., Carol Stream, Illinois 60188. All rights reserved.

Take note that the name satan and related names are not capitalized. We choose not to acknowledge him, even to the point of violating grammatical rules.

Soft cover ISBN: 978-0-9979923-6-6
eBook ISBN: 978-0-9979923-7-3

Library of Congress Cataloging-in-Publication Data
Names: Campbell, Samantha
Title: Fallen chains/Samantha Campbell;
LCCN: 2016958009
LC record available at https://lccn.loc.gov/2016958009

Cooke House Publishing
(a division of Cooke Consulting & Creations, LLC)
Winston-Salem, NC
publishing@cookecc.org

This book and all Cooke House Publishing books are available at Christian bookstores and distributors worldwide.

*Printed in the United States of America.*- First Edition

# CONTENTS

Acknowledgments 7

Foreword by Clydette Overton 9

Introduction 11

**Part 1: Bondage**

| | | |
|---|---|---|
| Chapter 1 | Lies from the Start | 15 |
| Chapter 2 | Teenage Love Affair | 19 |
| Chapter 3 | The Ultimate Heartbreak | 23 |
| Chapter 4 | Void Filler | 29 |
| Chapter 5 | For the Love of Honey | 35 |
| Chapter 6 | Incurable | 41 |
| Chapter 7 | Same Script, Different Cast | 47 |
| Chapter 8 | Sugar Daddy | 55 |
| Chapter 9 | Incarcerated: Prisoner of Love | 59 |
| Chapter 10 | New Address, Same Mess | 69 |
| Chapter 11 | False Positive | 75 |
| Chapter 12 | Rebound | 81 |

**Part 2: Freedom**

| | | |
|---|---|---|
| Chapter 13 | Changing Tide | 93 |
| Chapter 14 | Functionally Broken | 97 |
| Chapter 15 | Getting to the Root of What Ails You | 101 |
| Chapter 16 | Acceptance | 105 |

| Chapter 17 | Accountability | 109 |
| Chapter 18 | Forgiveness & Repentance | 113 |
| Chapter 19 | Bye Felicia, I Mean Shame | 119 |
| Chapter 20 | Taking Back Your Self-Worth | 123 |
| Chapter 21 | Growing Your Relationship with God | 135 |
| Chapter 22 | Finding Your Purpose | 147 |
| Chapter 23 | Discerning the Voice of God | 157 |
| Chapter 24 | Learning to Trust God | 163 |
| Chapter 25 | Waiting on God | 167 |
| Chapter 26 | This is War: Realizing Who the Real Enemy Is | 179 |
| Chapter 27 | Let Freedom Ring | 185 |

# ACKNOWLEDGMENTS

First and foremost, to the one who knew me before I was birthed into the earth, my Heavenly Father, thank you for choosing me to be a vessel for the uplifting of your Kingdom. I am nothing without You! When You call me home, I pray I've left everything that you've poured into me.

To my earthly father, although no longer here physically, I pray you are still watching over me and that your little girl has made you proud.

To my mommy, my best friend, and confidant, thank you for always believing in me, encouraging me, and covering me in prayer when I couldn't do so for myself. I am the woman I am because of the woman you are.

To my girls, my sistahs, whether you've been around with me from the beginning or just for a short while, I appreciate you! Thanks for doing life with me.

To my new husband, my happy place. I found freedom in writing this book, and when I found freedom, God sent me you. Thank you for being a part of my testimony and next chapter!

To my publisher, Tia Cooke, I could not have had a successful "delivery" without you. Thanks for being an amazing midwife!

Lastly, for every woman who wondered if she could ever be free, this book is for you! I hear the chains falling!

# FOREWORD

Samantha has shown a tremendous passion for putting words to paper all of her life. As her mom, I treasure the many letters, articles, and other sentiments she has written to me throughout her years. I remember carrying Samantha to church when she was two weeks old and my pastor placing his hands on her small head declaring that, "This child is blessed for greatness." Samantha has displayed these talents over and over throughout her life. It is through her expression of writing that she has been able to encourage friends and family alike. Outside of writing, Samantha possesses a natural light that attracts people to her, and this will be such a blessing for her desire to empower women. It is so gratifying to witness Samantha mature into the woman of God she is destined to become. Samantha has endured many hardships in life. One of the most devastating was the sudden death of her Dad when she was just 17 years old. Following the untimely death of her "Da," I watched her light dim a bit. In her grief, she would begin traveling a road that was not God-designed. As her mother, I'm blessed to know she has found her way back, realizing that God had a better plan for her life. By the Grace of God, she became strong enough to let go and let God. Samantha started to see herself as God sees her. She became able to focus on the new and wonderfully fulfilling relationship she had discovered with God. She has evolved into a very strong woman of God and continues to evolve even more each day. It is such an awesome pleasure to talk with her on a daily basis and witness the transformation God continues to bring about in her life. I am not only honored to call Samantha daughter but author. I pray God's richest blessings upon her.

-Clydette Overton

# INTRODUCTION

I struggled for many years with writing this book. Not because the writing was a challenge, but because the content would leave me transparently vulnerable and exposed. However, I've learned that my story is not mine to keep to myself but to share in the hopes that it will bless the life of another. For more than 6,570 days of my life, the enemy has been watering the seed of lies that he planted in me as a child. As you'll hear me mention in the book, he had an awareness of me and God's purpose for my life, long before I had an awareness of him. As I got older, the lie seed grew into a full-blown tree, with branches full of "lie limbs" that would drive me into a state of bondage attempting to suffocate the life out of me. But God! The enemy never intended for me to catch on to his scheme or reverse his tactic back on him, but there is a new sheriff in town!

In this book, I share with you intimate details of my story from bondage to freedom. The book is broken up into two sections: Bondage and Freedom. In the bondage section of the book, I will provide words of wisdom gleaned from each chapter of my story in bondage. You will also notice that a great deal of my story in bondage revolves around relationships with men. Please understand this is not about them, but about the avenue in my life that I used to find acceptance and worth that kept me in bondage. In the freedom section, I will outline for you my steps to becoming free. My prayer is that my story will speak to the heart of the woman who needs to be reminded that despite where she may have been or what she may have gone through, she is still God's Daughter of Promise. And she can be a Daughter of Freedom as God desires to free her from the chains of bondage and bring to fruition that which He purposed for her life. The Scripture says, *"Being confident of this very thing, that he which hath begun a good work in you will perform it until the day of Jesus Christ"* (Philippians 1: 6 KJV).

# PART 1

# BONDAGE

# CHAPTER 1

# LIES FROM THE START

*I sat on the doctor's table suddenly noticing that the only thing I could hear was the pounding of my heartbeat in my ears. I could see the doctor's mouth moving as she stood in front of me, but the sound of the words coming out of her mouth had ceased. Had I just heard her correctly? No, I couldn't have. Surely she'd mixed my file up with another patient. Ugh, why couldn't I hear her words anymore? I needed to hear her say she'd made a mistake. Please, God. Please. Not me.*

..................................................

*Let's go back to the beginning.*

The morning of my first day of 6th grade, I woke up with such anticipation of the new adventure that awaited me. Not only was I going to get to walk to school for the first time ever, but I was going to get to wear my slamming new baby blue wind suit, with the matching white and baby blue high-top Air Force 1 sneakers that I'd begged my parents to splurge on. Little did I know, but that day would prove to set the course for the next two decades of my life. I can remember walking out of the door with my lunch tray scouring the cafeteria for a seat. My eyes fell on a table with a group of girls who would have been considered the elite of our class. I noticed that there was one seat left, so I walked over to the table and sat down with them. As soon as I sat down, I heard one of the girls say, "Why is she sitting in 'so and so's' seat?" In that moment, it felt as though someone had punched me straight in the face. I felt so embarrassed and humiliated as I got up to go find another table to sit at. It was there that the enemy planted the seed of rejection and not feeling good enough—a seed that he would water and add gasoline to a burning fire for the next two decades.

Today, I realize that I was under attack from the enemy long before I even knew he existed. For as long as I can remember my mother has shared with me the fact that as a baby, the pastor told her that I was an anointed child. It was because of this that the enemy knew he couldn't waste any time sowing a seed that would try to derail the plan and purpose that God had for my life. He's been doing a good job up until now, but the tide has turned. That day in 6$^{th}$ grade would be the moment where the lie the enemy had sown would be used to dictate how I felt about myself for years to come. It seemed from that moment on, even subconsciously I was striving to find acceptance and approval that I was worthy or good enough to be chosen. One of the greatest quests for trying to find this acceptance would be through love and relationships with men. I had the preconceived notion that being chosen by a guy would dispel the myth about my not being good enough, but it wouldn't happen the way I envisioned at all. The enemy was going to use the thing I thought would make me feel better about myself to break me even further, that is until God freed me from the bondage of satan's lies. We'll talk about that later in the book— that's the most important part actually.

## *Words of Wisdom from Sam*

Some may read this chapter and think, "This girl is crazy to attach her issues to something that happened when she was 12 years old." However, I'd beg to differ. A negative perception of ourselves can likely be traced to a negative experience, even one that could have occurred decades earlier. I'll touch on this later in the book, but Scripture says, the enemy comes to steal, kill, and destroy (see John 10:10). Is it far-fetched to think he'd wait until you were 35 years old to plant his first seed of deception? No. By that time you could well be on your way to fulfilling God's purpose for your life, and that is a direct contradiction to what the enemy desires. If he can get you early, that gives him more time to fine-tune his craft and grow "lie limbs" to the tree of deception that would grow from the seed he planted. This is why I'd go so far to suggest that from the womb, parents should be praying and pleading the blood of Jesus over their children, mindful that all the enemy wants is to get his foot in the door when he can and where he can.

# CHAPTER 2

# TEENAGE LOVE AFFAIR

I was 16 the first time I realized men would be the way I tried to find a form of acceptance—it would start with a childhood friend. He was genuinely a nice guy, extremely handsome, so much so that I was excited to know he was even considering me. I can't exactly pinpoint where the "love affair" began, I just knew I was totally smitten with him. But what became clear was that I wasn't his only option. How do I know this? First, I attended a very small high school so it was rarely a secret about who was seeing who. Secondly, a few of the other girls and I would have conversations–including three-way calls–with them telling me the guy said he didn't like me. Thirdly, I had such loving friends who I could always count on to come back and say, "Did you know he took so and so to the house?" of which there was nothing I could do because he didn't belong to me. All of this seems so juvenile, but to a person who is seeking acceptance, it was truly crushing. I won't fault him for doing what seems natural for a teenage boy, but the game of "pick me, pick me"

was wearing on my 16-year-old spirit, and I was just about ready to accept defeat when it seemed as though the tide was changing.

I can remember seeing him at a fellow friend's birthday party not really wanting to even acknowledge his presence regardless of how I felt about him. However, whether I wanted to acknowledge him or not, he was going to get my attention, and he did so by pulling me to him and kissing me as though we weren't standing among a group of people. Maybe this should've made me feel confident in the fact that he cared for me, but it didn't. I needed more, and I was going to get that, in a sense. Not long after that event, he'd be graduating from high school. I can recall preparing to leave the graduation, and amongst all the commotion he grabbed me and invited me to his graduation party. I felt like a kid in a candy store, delighted that he would break away from one of the most special moments of his life to personally invite me to his party. He spent pretty much the entire party with me, and that night as he kissed me under the moonlight, I felt like something was shifting, like I was getting what I finally wanted from him. That would be the beginning of something wonderful. Although he hadn't given me a verbal commitment, I felt his actions were good enough to make me feel good enough. However, I wouldn't be able to bask long in "whatever" we were, before life would deal me a blow I wasn't prepared or equipped to deal with. The enemy was really preparing to flex his muscle.

### *Words of Wisdom from Sam*

*This word of wisdom is short and sweet: never make someone a priority who only considers you an option. In this part of my story, I'm talking about two teenagers, but this scenario is a common one even for adult women, including myself. We wait, and wait, and wait, for men to come around, then feel excited if and when they actually do, which is not always the case. As Daughters of Freedom, we need to be cognizant that if a man is having trouble deciding if we are the right one, we must help him out by solving the mystery for him and moving on. When a man wants you, and only you, you will not have to turn into a circus acrobat jumping through all sorts of hoops and hurdles. Point. Blank. And the Period.*

# CHAPTER 3

# THE ULTIMATE HEARTBREAK

I can still recall our very last conversation as though it happened yesterday and not 14 years ago. Every morning before I left the house for my summer job, I'd ask him for money. He'd normally hand me a five dollar bill, but that particular morning all he had was four, one dollar bills. I remember taking the bills out of his hands as we told each other, "I'll see you later." Never in a million years would I have thought that "later" would never come. While on break at my summer job, my manager came in to tell me to call home. I proceeded to do so and was informed that my uncle was very sick and my mom was on her way to pick me up. That call made me nervous — everyone knew how much I loved my uncle, yet something about the call didn't seem quite right, and it wasn't. Very soon I'd learn that the mention of my uncle was simply a decoy to protect me from reality for as long as possible. As I stood at the customer service desk attempting to retrieve my paycheck, my mother walked into the store.

I asked her if my uncle was okay and she proceeded to tell me, "Baby, daddy is gone." I had no idea what the crazy lady impersonating my mother was talking about. What did my father even have to do with anything? I continued with my task of retrieving my check. We walked out of the store, and I saw my aunt, uncle, and cousin standing outside of their car. I could hear them asking me if I was okay, yet I offered them no response. On the ride home, I remember leaning my head against the window thinking it was raining except the water on the window was inside— they were my tears, but why was I crying?

I was so glad to finally get home and see my father's car parked in the yard. "Da" (that's what I called him) was going to be so upset when I told him about the cruel thing momma said about him being gone. Inside the house, I saw so many people, so many except my Da. I can remember my cousin asking me if I wanted to walk out, and I agreed simply because there were just too many people in my house and I still couldn't understand why. On our walk out, we came upon a group of friends and all I kept hearing was, "Sam, I'm so sorry to hear about your dad." These people were making no sense to me, and I honestly felt uncomfortable. But seeing my— well I don't really know what to call him since he hadn't given me a verbal commitment—"special friend" in the midst of the crowd gave me great comfort. His embrace always made me feel safe, but this time there was something different about it, and his eyes held a sadness that I couldn't describe. Days passed and my home continued to be filled with people, all except my daddy. It was not like him to not even call.

I can remember one morning my mother coming to tell my siblings and me that we needed to go to the funeral home to pick out caskets. I'd been to the local funeral home before, but never to the back area where they kept the various casket styles. I could hear my family talking around me as we walked past casket after casket checking out different styles. All I could think was, "Who in the world died and why do they want us choosing caskets for them?" The evening of the wake, I can remember my mother telling me that I didn't have to go if I didn't want to, but how disrespectful would it have been to not pay respects to the family of whoever had died. Walking down the aisle of the funeral home I could hear people whispering, "I'm so sorry." and, "God Bless you, baby." I began looking around to find out who they were talking to as I felt it necessary to provide them my condolences as well. When I got to the front of the funeral home and looked into the casket, the sight before me made me weak in the knees. There in the casket lay my father. What was he doing in there? Was this some sort of cruel joke? Was Ashton Kutcher going to pop from behind the curtain at any minute telling me I'd been punk'd? Was this my daddy's way of getting back at me for acting like a spoiled brat at times? I couldn't understand what was happening. All I knew is that he looked so peaceful lying there, as though he was just napping and would awaken at any moment.

After the wake, I stood on our front porch feeling like someone whose skin had been rubbed raw. I could hear everyone around me having a good time, laughing and joking with one another, but I felt as though somebody had stolen my joy. I can remember my cousin asking my "special friend," "So, what's going on with you and my cousin?" In that moment, whatever breath I had left seemed to escape me. The last thing I needed that day was to feel rejected. I waited for what seemed like an eternity for his response, and when the words, "That's my girl." rolled off of his lips, I exhaled. He had chosen me—officially! I was good enough for him! And in that same moment, the enemy swept in with, "What type of person would he be to say you mean nothing to him when your father just died? Don't get excited."

The morning of the funeral there was so much activity swirling around me, but I felt like a fish out of water. The funeral home limo came to pick us up and I remember thinking I'd never rode in this car before, and why did I have to then. The church was overflowing with people expressing their love and appreciation for my father, but as I sat in the pew beside my mother, love nor appreciation was what I felt. What I felt was anger. The thought that kept racing through my mind was, "You told me you would see me later, not goodbye. You've never lied to me before." As the service was coming to a close, I heard the funeral officiate say, "We will now proceed with the final viewing of the body." *Final viewing? Was this the last time that I would lay my eyes on my father's face?* When the time came for the family's viewing, my legs seemed to have forgotten how to work. I can remember my cousin acting as an anchor for me by cuffing his arm into mine.

As I placed my favorite teddy bear in the casket, I stood there looking into a face that had become part of my existence for the past 16 years, the face of the first man I ever loved— it was at that moment that reality hit me. My daddy was gone. There would be no more drop-off and pick-ups from school, no more calling home asking him to bring me a barbeque sandwich from Shortstop for lunch, no more cracking watermelons and eating them on the back porch during summer, no more waking up in the middle of the night baking gingerbread cakes, no more "I'm proud of you" or "I love you baby girl." Who was going to walk me down the aisle and kiss my cheek before giving me away to my husband? The realization that my life was never going to be the same again caused the floodgate of tears to be broken. *Why, God, why? Why my daddy?* I found myself standing at his casket not crying, but wailing. My tears came from a place of hurt that I'd never experienced before. Loved ones tried to pull me away from the casket, but I needed just a few more seconds, just a few more seconds to touch the curls of his hair and the smoothness of his skin. Just a few more seconds to tell him how much I loved him. I needed just a few more seconds, just a few more to be my daddy's little girl.

### *Words of Wisdom from Sam*

*The only words of wisdom I can offer from this part of my story is to remember that grief is real, and it's okay to cry as much as you need to. Society has the tendency to sometimes categorize tears as a sign of weakness, but I believe God gave them to us as they hold much cleansing power. As you see from my story, I lost it at my father's casket, but I noticed that my mother never cried. The first week of his death she was too busy "entertaining" visitors and after that week too busy "entertaining" anything she could to not stop and sit with reality. My mother is a strong woman and the glue that kept my family together. I think she felt that if she lost it, what would happen to me. But what I don't think she realized is that her trying to actually hold it together was making her a shell of herself. Then one day God breathed on her, and the tears started to flow. In the midst of tears, I watched her come back to life. If you're grieving anything today whether it be the loss of a loved one, relationship, job, or something else, know that it is okay to cry.*

## CHAPTER 4

## VOID FILLER

Merriam-Webster defines *void* as an empty space.[1] Whenever there is some type of void one's natural instinct is to attempt to fill it (1) so that they don't have an empty hole inside of them, and (2) to numb the pain from the hurt the hole can cause. The day of my father's funeral I could feel the hole in my heart growing as his casket was lowered into the ground. After his passing, there was no denying a distinct void in my life, and my primary goal was to try and fill it. People use a wide array of void fillers including drugs, alcohol, and food. My choice of drug would be relationships and sex. After my father's passing, my first love and I continued to date, but it became no secret that my brokenness left me completely needy.

There came a point in our relationship, especially after he left for college, where things began to change. His weekends at home would end with me crying to the point of hyperventilation, not

---

1    Merriam-Webster. Accessed February 28, 2016. http://www.merriam-webster.com/dictionary/liability.

wanting him to leave, but knowing he had to. The only thing that would stop my tears would be him placing my head on his chest and telling me to breathe with the sound of his heartbeat. His heartbeat had become my heartbeat, and at that point in my life, he was the only man I had left to truly love me. But he could only love me from a distance, and that is where I believe the strain and tension crept into our relationship. Our nightly phone calls and sporadic weekend visits were not filling the void and numbing the pain of my father's death, so my eyes began to fixate on the next best thing who could—someone who was local. The issue was not that I no longer loved my boyfriend because I did. In fact, I practically fought to get him to be mine. As long as I was filling the void in my heart, I was okay, but even the slightest inkling that there was unfilled space caused things to go bad.

The new guy was a childhood friend whom I already had a certain level of trust for so it wasn't hard for me to allow him in to fill the part of the void that my first love was no longer able to occupy. To some it would seem crazy and selfish to allow two men to occupy my heart, but during that time I honestly did not care. I knew that I wasn't a cold-hearted person, and being unfaithful was not my m.o., but all I cared about was making sure the void was completely filled at all times. If it wasn't, then that left room for me to feel the pain of my father's absence, and I by no means wanted to feel that pain—I just wasn't equipped to deal with it. My juggling the two of them went on for about a year before things started to spiral out of control. I was beginning to not be able to keep my lies straight, and things were soon about to come to a head.

I can remember vividly the night the two exchanged slight words in front of all our friends. After the (thankfully) brief exchange of words, I chased behind my love not believing it had come to this because of me. When I caught up to him the expression on his face told me his pride had been bruised and what we used to be, we would be no more. It was never my intention to cause him any undue pain, but the saying is true, "hurt people, hurt people." A substance abuse user doesn't intentionally desire to harm their loved ones by stealing from them to get money for their drug habit, all they know is that they have to keep the hurting place inside of them filled. As much as I was going to miss my first love, my greater concern was what I was going to do to fill the part of the void he occupied. Luckily enough, I didn't have to worry about that, because instead of only occupying half, the new guy's presence filled the entire void, and did so for several years. During the years we were together he showered me with physical and emotional affection as well as all the material things a girl could ask for. He, in my eyes, had indeed become a true replacement for my father. I had never felt such a "happy" place during the years we were together, but the expiration date on that "happy" place would soon be reaching its end date.

    Things in our relationship started taking a turn for the worse as my neediness began to suffocate us. The two of us living three hours apart was okay with me initially, but towards the end of our relationship I needed him with me 24/7, but he couldn't do that at that time. Visits that once used to be joy filled became tension filled and ending with my crying and begging him mercilessly not to leave me. I could feel the distance between us growing and the hole in my heart opening back up. That was not an option for me. I knew he loved kids so I decided to conjure up a false pregnancy and false miscarriage to make him feel sorry enough to stay with me. In my mind, I didn't care how disgusting that decision was, desperate times called for desperate measures and I couldn't have him leave me. After my faked miscarriage, things did seem to go back to the way they were in the beginning, and yet again I felt a place of happiness. However, this would only be very temporary. I'd "played" all the cards I had for the situation between him and me. I couldn't hold on to us any longer, but I also couldn't have the hole in my heart exposed.

I had no idea what I was going to do. I opted to try going back to my first love. What we had was special and I didn't think he was seeing anyone, so surely he'd be open to at least trying to reconcile. When approaching my first love with my proposition for reconciliation, his response wasn't a flat out no, but what I learned really quickly was that those two lovesick teenagers no longer existed. What had taken their place was a man desiring my honey (sex), and my desire to give it to him just to keep the plug in the hole in my heart.

It was bittersweet for me to realize that my first love was no longer concerned with what was inside of my heart, but what was between my legs. What was even more bittersweet is that I had made him that way. I longed for the emotional connection that we once had so I used a low ball effort like I did with the last guy. I told him that when we were together I'd gotten pregnant and lost the babies. I decided to pull the twin number with him hoping for extra sympathy points, explaining that's why some of my behavior was the way it was. It appeared that made him sympathetic to the situation but didn't change his desire to want to be connected to me emotionally. It saddened me to see what we had become, but I still needed his presence as at least a piece of a void filler. However, that too would only be short-lived.

My intuition was telling me that another female had taken my place in his heart and this was confirmed for me after this one-liner, "Samantha, you are the reason she and I can't be happy. You are in the way." At that moment, I couldn't figure out what was worse, trying to have the void filled by someone I couldn't ever fathom would say something like that to me, or dealing with the loss of my father. I wasn't prepared to deal with the latter. At that point, I realized I didn't care about love or relationships anymore, they just added to my pain. Instead, I'd just used my newfound tool—my honey—to fill my void.

### *Words of Wisdom from Sam*

*Dealing with grief, and being in the state of bereavement has the ability to change a person's character. For most, the first year after the loss of a loved one, you're just not thinking clearly. Some people are able to move through the grief process with ease, but then there are some like myself who get stuck in the first phase—denial. When a person gets stuck in this phase, they have to find a way to fill the void of losing their loved one, simply because facing reality is just unthinkable. Writing this chapter was hard for me because I had to come clean about some of the horrible things I did like being unfaithful to my partner or stooping so low as to falsify pregnancies to try and make someone love me and keep the hole in my heart filled. I fully own my decisions and don't excuse my behavior. However, I just know that when you're grief-stricken, the desire to not hurt another is overshadowed by your own desire to not feel hurt. As I said above, hurt people, hurt people.*

# CHAPTER 5

# FOR THE LOVE OF HONEY

It has been said that one of the most powerful tools a woman possesses is her "honey." Honey is supposed to be sweet and addictive making it hard to resist when placed in front of you. My thought process was that after one dip in my honey, whoever the man was in my life at that time would have no choice but to want to be around. To put the icing on the cake, I'd even allow him to dip into my honey without any form of protection since I'd heard sex felt better for a man without a condom. That would surely make him stay and my void issue wouldn't be an issue. I'd hear consistently how sacred my "honey" was and how it should be cherished— at one time I believed that, but at this point in my life it had simply become a tool to mask my pain. During that time in my life, in the eyes of everyone, it seemed like I was doing exceptionally well getting over my father's death. On the surface I was excelling in college, holding down a job, and playing the good little church girl, but behind the scenes, I was spiraling downward. No one would think I was doing so great if they could see the person I turned into behind closed doors. When the sun went down, and even sometimes while it was still up, I turned into a modern-day Jezebel.

My first rock bottom year took place about 5 years after my father passed. I was facing some serious financial challenges (because taking care of my business financially was far from my mind), and so I thought it was a blessing to have found a job that was flexible enough to accommodate my class schedule. On the surface I was a true professional, but underneath I was "jonesing" badly because no one was currently filling the hole in my heart at that time. The day of my job interview I can recall walking into the establishment and laying my eyes on a gentleman who was just my type—tall, dark, and handsome. He smiled at me and the deep baritone filled words, "How you doing?" falling from his lips sent shivers down my spine. When he walked past me, the scent of his cologne dulled my senses. From that point on every time we would cross each other's path there would be unspoken words, until one day those words became verbalized. It's amazing how the words, "if you think you're grown" can spark trouble. The first day he came over to my apartment our interaction was more playful and flirtatious. As he had me pinned against the wall the moonlight peeking through the blinds kissed his chiseled jawline and I knew without a doubt that he would be my next void filler.

The first time we would take our "relationship" from friends to "friends with benefits" would come only a few months after I started the new job. I think I should put a pin here and note that not long after I started the job I became aware that he had a long-term girlfriend who also worked at our job. Now a normal person with any shred of moral decency would never charter into such territory. Even I knowing the person I used to be, would never think of sleeping around with another woman's man, but I wasn't the person I used to be and I didn't care about anyone's feelings besides my own. Remember, hurt people, hurt people. Our booty call sessions (forgive my vulgarity, but I have to call them what they were since none of our interactions occurred before 11 PM) would go on for months. Oddly enough each session with him was better than the last, and I became a true addict looking for my next fix. I felt no pain. I heard someone say that an addict is always looking for a fix that is better than the last— I guess that would be no exception for me. His presence through sex was filling the void in my heart, but much like past situations, my neediness began to kick in and I desired something more and began to express this to him. In my mind, it wouldn't be an issue considering how much he told me he enjoyed the sex. Ladies, let me put a pin right here that I will address later in the book. A man saying he enjoys having sex with you does not equate to him loving you.

After our first conversation about my wanting more, I knew my thought process had been very wrong. I knew I wanted more, but I wasn't willing to risk pushing the issue and making his desire to end the only "situationship" (sexual relationship) we had together. He had been a great void filler and I couldn't risk losing that. I can recall the night he fell asleep resulting in him spending the entire night with me. I was so happy that the following morning I was up fixing a full course breakfast only for him to come out of the bedroom telling me he didn't want any. In my mind, that equated to his saying, "Don't forget this is just sex." I was truly grasping at straws that equated to having a warm body in my bed for a couple of hours a night. After countless "sex escapade" nights, I realized that I desired someone to replace the hole left in my heart from my father's passing, but my father's presence in my life never left me feeling empty like I had begun to fill at that point in my life. I was truly becoming a shell of myself.

During the course of the *situationship* between my co-worker and I, one of my ex-boyfriends came back on the scene. I knew at one point he truly adored me, so my hope was that he would bring with him the emotional component that I was desperately lacking. However, it wouldn't be long before I realized he, too, was only interested in sex. I was sick of using my honey as a tool, but it was all I had. I was sinking, sinking, sinking. For the first time in my life, I'd begun sleeping with two men at the same time. It seemed as though one would be coming in the front door, while the other was heading out the back. There would be nights where I'd still have the stench of sex from one of them when the other would come over to rise between my thighs. What had I become? Who was this person? I felt like somebody rotting on the inside. I needed to be in the presence of someone I knew truly loved me, so my mother came to visit.

### *Words of Wisdom from Sam*

*If you ask me today, I will quickly tell you that I have no desire to have someone else's stuff, and when I reference "stuff" I mean another woman's man. However, as you can see from my story, that was not always the case. As much as I pin my poor judgment on my grief, I still have to take some accountability (which we will dig into in the "freedom" section of the book). As selfish as it is to say, the only person's feelings I cared about back then were my own. When I would see his girlfriend, I wish I could say I felt bad about sleeping with her man, but I didn't. In fact, I was so reckless, I thought I had more to offer than her, and eventually he would see that, but he did not. Allow me to offer a couple of pieces of wisdom here. Regardless of the reasons behind why we do things, whatever we sow, we will reap. I am certain karma has paid me a few visits for what I did to her and I cannot be upset about that. I also can't speak to anyone's situations but mine, and in my case the guy did not leave his girlfriend as I thought in my mind he would, so this made me the side-chick. As Daughters of Freedom, we should value ourselves enough to know we deserve to be the only, not the other. We should also value our sisters enough to not touch things that don't belong to us. If their significant other comes sniffing around our way, we do not have to respond or act on their advances-we have a choice.*

*In this chapter, you also hear me mention sleeping with two men at the same time. This is a 100% absolute judgement free zone, and I know we're living in a time where women don't want the double standard that says it's wrong for a woman to "get hers," but I will say this: Scripture tells us that our bodies are our temple, and when we sleep with people, in general, we take in their spirit. Sleeping with multiple men does not say I value myself or my body, and it should also shed light on why some of us struggle with internal peace; there are too many spirits fighting inside of you, when the only one that should be there is the Holy Spirit (I'll dig into this subject a bit more in a later chapter).*

## CHAPTER 6

## INCURABLE

My mother's two-week visit was a welcomed one as I truly felt like I was spinning out of control. Having her around cured my emotional distress, but physically I was not well. I'd begun experiencing severe pain in my rear end and burning when I urinated. One night I can remember sharing with my mother how I felt and she suggested I soak in a warm bath. While soaking in a bath one evening, I asked her to come into the bathroom and tell me if she saw anything. She looked at me with a blank stare and simply said, "I think you should get checked out by your doctor, baby." The tone of her voice in that comment didn't quite sit well with me so I decided to google my symptoms. I refused to believe what my Google searches were saying, after all, self-diagnosing was so dangerous.

I didn't immediately take my mother's advice to seek my physician, but as the days went on the pain I'd been experiencing became more severe—so severe that I ended up in Urgent Care. At the Urgent Care, the doctor asked me what symptoms I was experiencing. After telling her my symptoms, she asked if I'd been sexually active without the use of condoms. I, unfortunately, had to tell her yes, many times over in fact. At that point, she told me that she needed to do a pelvic exam. I'd always hated pelvic exams, but this particular one was not right. My glands were so swollen the doctor was not even able to get the cervical clamp inside me without causing severe pain. Not wanting to continue causing me pain, she finally ended up checking the outside only where she found a sore on the outer part of my vagina. Her next words sounded like fingernails scraping against a chalkboard, "Ms. Overton, we will need to cut a piece of the sore off for testing." She needed to cut a piece of flesh off of one of the most sensitive body parts that in my case was already inflamed. Having her cut off a piece of the sore was one of the most physically painful experiences I'd ever had in my life. Waiting for the doctor to return seemed like an absolute eternity. My mind was racing all over the place, especially after realizing I'd been walking around with a sore on my private parts. That was not normal, and I knew it.

    Roughly 20 minutes later the doctor came back into the office and as long as I live, I will never forget her words. She said to me, "Ms. Overton, I'm very sorry to have to tell you this, but it looks like you've contracted genital herpes. We're going to send the sample off, but I'm pretty certain." At that moment, I calmly began running off questions like how, and when could I have contracted it. I told her that I always looked at my partner's genitalia and I never saw any sores or any evidence of anything being wrong. She informed me that I was likely exposed less than a month prior to my visit. She further explained to me that men didn't need outer sores since they could pass it through their semen. She went on to say to me, "Ms. Overton, you seem pretty calm. You are aware that herpes is an incurable sexually transmitted disease, correct? It's not potentially fatal like the AIDS virus, but we can only treat it, not cure it. Do you know who you may have contracted it from?" That question sent me over the edge, turning my calm demeanor into one of anger. "I DON'T KNOW WHICH ONE IT WAS!" I screamed at her.

In that moment, I wasn't angry with the doctor, I was angry with me. Based on her timeline, I couldn't pinpoint specifically who it was. Why? Because I'd slept with two men in the same night, without protection. The night in question, I didn't even have time to wash the first guy off of me, before the next guy was coming through my door. In that moment, I felt my breath escaping me. The doctor prescribed Valtrex to help with the outbreak I was experiencing. To be honest, I cannot remember how I drove myself from the Urgent Care to the pharmacy. I remember sitting at the pharmacy having to call my mother and lie to her about what was wrong with me so that she could give me the money to pay for my prescription. I couldn't bear telling her what the prescription was really for. I sat in the pharmacy lobby thinking about how only a few days ago I'd saw a commercial for a couple with herpes and how I mocked them looking so happy about living with an STD. I was in so much physical pain sitting there, but more than that, I was in so much emotional pain because I'd been sleeping with two different men within hours and I could not honestly pinpoint which one of them gave it to me. How was that possible? Who was this person?

After the diagnosis, my life no longer became about trying to mask the pain from the loss of my father, it became about trying to mask the pain of feeling completely worthless. Here, the enemy had attached a huge "lie branch" to his tree of lies in my life. My desire to be loved and to feel good enough went to an entirely different level. I, of course, had to share the news with the two guys in question. They both denied their having it. I was pretty certain one of them had not given it to me as we'd slept together many times when we'd dated years back, and disease was never an issue. However, the other gentleman–well since I was his side chick–I'd think it would be safe to say his integrity could be questionable. Oddly enough, that wouldn't matter because two weeks later he'd be standing in my bedroom again. The night he showed up at my door unannounced, I should have put up a fight, but I let him in as though all was well with the world. When he stepped inside my apartment, the words, "I'm sorry" rolled off of his lips. My ears perked, thinking perhaps I was preparing to receive a confession from him. "I would never put you in that type of situation," he went on to say. He stood over me whispering words in my ear that had caused me more trouble than I'd ever bargained for: "I still want you." Even with his denial that he was the one who gave me the virus, I was sure it was him. How could I possibly have even considered allowing him to touch me again, but in that moment, those three words—I want you—held so much irony because I needed to feel wanted more than ever, even if from the person who infected me in the first place. "I can spend the night if you want me to." And with those words, the fight I hadn't bothered to put up in the first place was gone. Pressed against the wall, his lips moved from my ear, down to my chest. When I looked over his shoulder a tear escaped my eye as I saw the pill bottle of Valtrex sitting on my dresser. *My God, what was I doing?* I was on a downward spiral, completely broken ... shattered ... and it was just getting started.

### *Words of Wisdom from Sam*

*One of the things I have learned over the course of my life is that we as women do not take enough responsibility for the health of our sexual bodies. As you can see from my own story I wasn't being accountable for protecting myself. I believe so much responsibility has been placed on the man to provide protection, but it should be the woman's responsibility as well simply because she should value and honor herself enough to not allow anybody inside her body without protection. Many times, and I speak from personal experience, we don't require men to wear condoms because they don't think it "feels as good." The act of participating in unprotected sex poses so many threats, yet I think many, including myself, simply think the inevitable could never happen to them. For me, I was so emotionally disturbed I even thought pregnancy wouldn't have been bad and would have given me a lifetime attachment to someone. Contracting an incurable disease never crossed my mind. I was such a hot mess, I used to feel honored to have a man ejaculate in my body, not having to pull out. Surely they'd think I was that much more special.*

*As a Christian woman who now lives a life of celibacy, I don't promote premarital sex, but if you choose to participate in sex, I cannot stress enough the importance of protecting yourself. Birth control only helps prevent pregnancy, not sexually transmitted diseases. Not only does having unprotected sex put you at risk for sexually transmitted diseases, it also puts you at risk for getting the Human Papilloma Virus (HPV). This virus is pretty common for most sexually active women, but it puts the woman at risk of getting cervical cancer. Because I am also a carrier of HPV, I have had PAP smears that come back abnormal. In some cases, precancerous cells will be found on my cervix and I will have a not so comfortable procedure to biopsy a piece of my cervix. When I think about how unprotected sex has changed my life, I realize that my health and wellbeing should have been more important than a man's desire to "feel the real thing." As a matter of fact, I'm now a firm believer that couples should get tested for sexually transmitted diseases together. Someone who has nothing to hide will oblige. Know your status and theirs. It's your life and your health.*

## CHAPTER 7

# SAME SCRIPT, DIFFERENT CAST

"Really? You're ok with it?" That would become a standard question for me after the herpes diagnosis, after which I would proceed to pull my panties down to allow yet another man to enter my body simply because he didn't run immediately. My longing for love had begun to no longer just be about the passing of my father, but the need to feel worth something to somebody. The herpes diagnosis left me feeling disgusting and worthless and I needed to figure out a way to make those feelings go away. I'd go back to what was familiar—men. Regardless of what I thought about myself, I vowed to always be honest about the condition. The first time I told a man, I can remember sitting and waiting for the inevitable when the word *herpes* would roll off of my lips. I would wait to hear the words, "You're a disgusting whore," but ironically those words never came. In fact, those words never came from any man I ever told. At least not verbally. My level of neediness hit an all-time high after the diagnosis and for every man who said they were okay with the condition. I dug my claws in, needing to hold on to them by any means necessary so I'd feel validated. However, what I was really doing was being violated. I started to believe that the men who told me it was okay thought they had an opportunity to get whatever they wanted from me because hey, I should have just been grateful they decided to stay. Not every man would be so kind. Let me note here that no man ever verbally said that to me. That is the "lie limb" the enemy embedded in my mind. I found myself in situations where I'd get off the phone with "baby mamas" claiming they were still together and I'd tell myself, "It's not that bad," just so I wouldn't have to let go. I'd allow men to show up at my house at obscene times of the night because "anytime was better than no time" and I couldn't rock the boat for fear they'd change their mind. I'd become their personal ATM giving them money hand over fist. Not paying my own bills so that I could send money to them via Western Union. In my mind, I could buy their loyalty. A part of me knew the behavior I was accepting from those men was despicable, but the larger part of me couldn't let go.

During the era when Facebook really started to pop, I found myself talking to a guy through a mutual Facebook group. He was an older gentleman, but so, so handsome. Back then my self-esteem was so low that if you were any type of handsome and looking my way I was all in. He started saying all the right things, coupled with the "I've fallen on hard times. Can you possibly help me out?" spiel. At that time in my life, it was an "honor" to feel needed, and like past times perhaps I would show him how "ride or die" I was and he would "wife" me. Let me put a pin here and note that this guy was in another state, and the only form of communication we'd had was through social media, yet I was willing to give him my hard-earned money. Because he was only in the next state over, South

Carolina, we discussed meeting in-person which I'd later find out was just an act of him blowing smoke up my wazoo to pacify me. After sending him hundreds of dollars to help him "get back on his feet," I convinced my friend to take a mini-vacation with me to the town where he resided. One positive thing I can say about this story is that he was truthful about where he resided and worked. I decided to surprise him at the nightclub he worked at and boy was he ever surprised. When he saw me, he wasn't rude. In fact, we took pictures together with the promise of us getting together the next day to spend time outside of his work. Well, we stayed in the town for another two days and I didn't hear a mumbling word. Should I have been surprised? No. But was I surprised? Yes. I felt very hurt behind that situation especially given the fact that I'd dished out money to a man I barely knew based on false promises. Perhaps you'd think I'd learned my lesson, but I hadn't.

One day a blast from the past came back into my life. He and I were so close as children, but I had no idea that as adults he would add to my broken state of being. When we reconnected I just knew it was fate. He truly appeared to be a breath of fresh air compared to the other men I'd encountered in the previous few years. I told him about the herpes diagnosis and he was so kind about it. He was a keeper in my book, so when I started to notice that he was experiencing some financial difficulties, it was a no-brainer that I'd offer to help him out. Again, I thought my money would buy his loyalty. I started shelling out money left and right, convincing myself that he would have to see what an "asset" I was to his life. I was so enamored with how well things were going, I neglected to notice that while I was supporting him financially, my own bills were stacking up. We'd not established a "formal" relationship because he thought it would be difficult with us being states apart. However, the distance didn't matter to me, and if I was going to be in debt behind him, I deserved a title. The title he was willing to give me was "friend but …" This title was supposed to mean we were friends, but we were also a little more. I tried to convince myself that I was okay with that, but I wasn't. I was under the impression that even though we didn't have a formal title, we still had a level of commitment to each other that meant we would only be involved with each other. It was nothing for us to go months and not see each other. My friends kept telling me that if he wasn't getting it from me, he was getting it from somewhere, but I couldn't believe this. I trusted him. Lo and behold something was on the horizon that would once again shake my being.

During a conversation with my cousin, she asked me if the guy had another child, a toddler. My response to her was he had a child, but the child was much older than a toddler. My cousin directed me to where she saw the photos—Instagram. It was, in fact, true. He did have a small child that he neglected to tell me about in all the conversations we'd had over the past almost two years. How could he forget to tell me something like that? I'll tell you why. It would prove that he'd been deceitful, lying to me about what he was really doing. Perhaps I should have listened to my cousin and not been so naïve about thinking we were both only dealing with each other, but I only wanted to see the good in him. I don't even know if I was so much disturbed by another child, but by the incident where he'd asked me for money to help for a baby shower for his God-child which was likely a lie—the money was more likely than not for the baby shower of his own child. I soon realized all the money I gave him did not buy his loyalty, further fueling the fire for his betrayal. I was heartbroken and financially broken and truly in a state of "Lord, I need you to just help me get through the moment" because anything outside of each moment was too hard to think about.

## *<u>Words of Wisdom from Sam</u>*

*For many years I lived by the notion that if I emptied out my pockets monetarily for men, they would realize how much of a "hold your man down" woman I was. This mindset is truly that of a person who does not know her worth. I'm not judging or looking down on women who choose to give a man money, but what I do want to stress is that a person who really loves you and wants you in their life, will make that known without you having to bend over backwards to show them how "valuable" you are by acting as their personal bank. The saying money can't buy love is not just a cliché—it's fact. It is not uncommon today to see the roles reversed in many relationships, where the woman now takes care of the man. We as women have taken on the role as the "provider" as a means of keeping the man around. Note I said "we" as I am no exception. Today, in hopes of coercing a man to love us, we ride men around in our passenger seats, give them keys to places where they pay no bills (and wouldn't even if they had the means to), pay their child support for them, give them money to help them get back on their feet, and the list goes on. God created Eve to be Adam's helpmate, not his ATM. Giving men money or putting yourself in financial distress will not make them desire to be with you anymore if they have not already had that plan in mind.*

*I've sacrificed my financial health, giving away money to men so that they could be okay, while my bills went unpaid. I can recall instances where I wasn't giving out $10 or $15 dollars rather $50's and $100's all because my self-worth was so low. I thought that giving them money would show how valuable I was to their lives. Please hear me when I say that you should never, ever have to give a man money to show him your worth. A man of significant caliber will not even feel right taking your money, at least not long-term. He will be invested in trying to do everything* *in his power to figure out how to make his situation better. Note I say, "his" situation. Now don't get me wrong, I believe that in a marriage, there may be instances where the wife has to carry more financial responsibility temporarily for various reasons, perhaps an unforeseen layoff of the husband's job or he falls unexpectedly ill. Please note that I say "marriage" here, this is a different covenant than a relationship. The act of giving boyfriends husband privileges is an entirely different discussion.*

*I'd also like to offer another piece of wisdom gleaned from my story. There is nothing wrong with desiring a commitment from someone who says they genuinely care for you and want you in their life. When men start tossing around the idea that a title doesn't mean anything as long as the two of you know what it is, please understand that is bologna. A man who has nothing to hide, and knows what a treasure he has in you, will have no problem sharing with the world that you all are exclusive. I often hear much controversy around social media and people's relationship statuses. Allow me to say that from my own experience, whenever a guy gave me a hard time about changing his relationship status or sharing photos of us on social media there was always a reason, and the main one being they had something else going on.*

*I believe the ultimate commitment is marriage which is honored in the eyes of God. Many times as women we are quick to hand out husband privileges to boyfriends or less under the guise of if I show him that I'm wife material he will actually make me one. I often hear the phrase, "why buy the cow when you can get the milk for free?" If you are already acting like a man's wife as his girlfriend, is there a real incentive or rush on his part for that situation to change? You know the saying, "why mess up a good thing." A while back a guy friend told me that men know in less than a year whether they see a future with a woman or not, so giving men years to decide could possibly be a waste of time. Remember, time is precious and this is the show, not a rehearsal.*

## CHAPTER 8

# SUGAR DADDY

"Bitch, give me my fucking phone. You don't be going through my shit," he said snatching his cell phone out of my hand. I stood in the middle of my bedroom floor trying to register the words that had just come out of his mouth. I'd never think the day would come where I'd be called a bitch, let alone from my boyfriend. Perhaps I should share some context leading up to this event. After things ended in my last "situationship" where I was left emotionally and financially broken, I thought I had a sense of, "I know what I deserve." So I ended up in a relationship with a guy who was perfect on paper: handsome, wealthy, and didn't spare any expense on me. It felt like a breath of fresh air to have someone pull their wallet out to give me money, instead of to put my money in. He was also two decades older than me, but that didn't matter. I was so "honored' to have a guy like that think I was "worthy" of loving.

We lived in two different cities, but with him working in the city where I lived we spent pretty much every weekday together. But then there was the weekend. Something odd would happen on the weekend. My boyfriend and I never spent the weekend together. I'd often speak to him on Friday before he drove back home, but once he got home, there was no communication. Sometimes he'd tell me he was going to be busy doing odd tasks and may not be available by phone, other times he wouldn't tell me anything and I just wouldn't be able to reach him again until Monday. Then there was the issue of my never having been to his home. He did live in a different city, but it wasn't far enough that I shouldn't have been invited there especially as his girlfriend.

I ended up having a conversation about my concerns with him and he pulled the age card on me. You know the one that goes something like this: "This is where our age difference shows. At my age, the things you are concerned with don't concern me, but that doesn't mean I'm cheating. I'm with you almost every weekday for goodness' sake." And indeed he was. I'd never dated an older man so perhaps what he cited regarding our age difference and the variation in what concerned us was true. These things still came off as red flags to me, but at that place in my life, I really couldn't tell the difference between insecurity and intuition. I didn't really want to "rock the boat" too much because outside of the red flags he was good to me.

Then something happened. One night as we lay on the couch watching television a phone started to ring. This seemed really odd considering both of our cell phones were sitting on the coffee table in front of us. I remember telling him his pocket was ringing and his response to me was, "That's your phone." After I promptly reminded him that both our phones were on the coffee table, he said that it was indeed his second cell phone used only for his daughter to call. Perhaps I could have stretched to believe this, but the caller kept calling, and I don't believe a parent would ignore their child's call, especially if they're calling back to back. Big red flag.

My suspicions grew considerably after that point. One night while he was in the shower I went through his things to try and find the "suspect" cell phone to no avail. I went to his car and found the phone in his console. The phone was powered off. When it powered up, there were back to back calls from the same phone number. Once again my thought was he would never leave a phone that was designated for his daughter in his car. I also began to think about the area code. It was the same area code for the location where he claimed his car broke down over Valentine's Day weekend. He told me the reason I wasn't able to reach him was because he forgot to get his cellphone out of his car before the tow truck took it. That night when I went back in the house, he looked different to me. Something was off, very off. The entire night I couldn't rest with the information I'd found earlier. My curiosity got so bad that when he was in the bathroom the following morning, I took it upon myself to go through the phone he had brought in the house with him. Except this time I wouldn't have enough time to go through it before he caught me, which brings us to the scenario at the beginning of the chapter. The person that I saw that morning was not the person I'd come to know over the last year. That person was cold and defensive. Granted, I should not have been going through his things, but it was his reaction that told me everything I needed to know. It wasn't my insecurity—my intuition was right.

### *Words of Wisdom from Sam*

*I could likely give more detail from the story above, but I think you may be able to get the gist. During that phase of my life, I was still very much in the "feeling worthless" zone and if a man was okay with my herpes announcement we were good. With this guy I felt like I truly hit the jackpot because not only was he okay with my condition, he gave me everything I wanted materialistically. But I hadn't hit the jackpot, he was a cheater. Many times when we don't completely understand our worth, we feel the need to pick and choose what being treated well looks like. For example, in my case, my herpes made me feel like I should have been grateful to have such a "great" guy be interested in me and the fact that he was good to me financially was an added bonus. But I deserved more than that, more like fidelity. As Daughters of Freedom, we should not be in scenarios where we say, "He takes care of me financially, but he abuses me or he is a chronic cheater. Or he is monogamous, but won't work or help contribute to the household." There should be a balance.*

## CHAPTER 9

# INCARCERATED: PRISONER OF LOVE

I sat in the visitation room looking around at the guards standing on post in each corner, their faces had grown familiar over the course of my bi-weekly, and sometimes weekly visits to the prison. It didn't matter how many times I came, I never grew comfortable with the strict environment—I always felt on edge. That was at least until the love of my life at the time walked through the door. Even in such a dark place, his presence in the room always made me feel safe. I remember the first time I met him, he was what I considered a gentleman with a bad boy side. I've always been a sucker for that type. Our "summer of love" would be interrupted by life, and I wasn't sure I'd ever see him again. But then life would reconnect us, just not in the best circumstances. During the ten years that we lost touch with one another, I'd think of him, but something would be different in 2011. As I drove to work one morning, he fell on my mind in the heaviest way. I began to ask friends if they knew whatever happened to him. None of my friends knew, so I resulted to the one place that becomes a default when you can't find a person—the department of corrections website. Sure enough there I'd find him. I told myself I didn't want to start communicating with an inmate so I'd just write him, but not long after that conversation with myself, he fell on my mind again in the heaviest way. I concluded that perhaps this was God telling me to reach out to him, so I did.

When we reconnected he was in the process of not yet having served even half of a 12-year prison sentence. This saddened me because I knew I had no plans on getting into anything serious with someone who was incarcerated. I told myself that I would just try to support him as a friend, but then something happened. Before our reconnection, I'd spent the previous year trying to recover from some of the blows I'd been dealt in my quest to feel I was loveable, but I was still by no means healed. I knew I was saved, but my relationship with God had been one lacking a certain level of intimacy, so I was working on that as well as hearing His voice. I was still so starved for love. So much so that entering into a relationship with a man who was incarcerated for more than a decade didn't seem like a bad idea after all. I'd convinced myself that being in a relationship with him was what God desired. Yes, I'd be a martyr for the cause and God would get the glory from our story. We would be a testimony to the world of how God could sustain you even in the most difficult times. Even in what seemed to be a dark and lonely place, I began to watch love grow and change the both of us. I honestly had never seen a connection like the one we shared. The beauty of it was that the connection was not based on anything physical because we'd never given each other anything more than hugs and small pecks on the lips. I had been allowing my body to be misused for so long, it felt refreshing to connect with someone on a deeper level—a level so deep that even if he wanted to, he would not be able to have my body.

I've always been a person who appreciated thoughtful gifts and oddly enough that is what I got from him—homemade cards, flower bouquets made out of potato chip bags, and handwritten letters with the scent of his cologne. I took heed to all the voices of those around me cautioning me to be aware that those in prison could attempt to manipulate people to get what they wanted. I knew this and had heard of these stories, but never felt that was the case with him. He never asked me to give him anything. I willingly put money on his commissary to try and make his living arrangement as pleasant as it could be. I consistently kept money on my phone so that we could speak at least once a day sometimes more on the weekend. I was over the moon excited when he told me there was a possibility for him to get his sentence reduced which meant his coming home to me sooner than anticipated, it would just require obtaining a good lawyer. I didn't care that the lawyer would take more than $1,000 out of my pocket—I considered it to be an investment into our future.

I remember the day he asked me to marry him during one of our visits. The proposal was not the one I dreamed of, you know the one where my love would sweep me off to a romantic getaway and propose on one knee on the beach under a star-filled sky. No, this proposal was much different. His getting on one knee was out of the question unless we wanted the guards to end our visit early from his disobedient act of moving from the position he was supposed to sit in for the duration of our two-hour visit. My proposal was simple. He took my hand, looked me in my eyes, told me how much he loved me, and asked me to be his wife. His wife in prison. But did that matter? No. It wasn't the perfect situation, but it seemed like the perfect love, so my answer was yes. After the visit, that afternoon I was tickled roaming the aisles of Charming Charlie, in the quest to find a "placeholder" engagement ring, you know just one until he could get out and get me a real one. He had given me instructions for what to do to start the marriage approval process. This wouldn't be just a simple case of us deciding to marry, we would need to have it approved by the prison institution. That bothered me a bit. Why did someone other than God have to approve our desire to commit to each other for life? However, I put my disgruntled feelings aside and proceeded to write my letter to the prison warden explaining why we should be allowed to marry—he would be doing the same. Two weeks later, I received a letter from the prison informing me that our request for marriage had been approved and the date set. I was getting married! And I was happy ... I thought.

A few weeks later we would hear back about the proceedings regarding having his sentenced reduced. There would be a reduction, but not by much, roughly 11 months. I don't think I was prepared for that blow. I'd held such hope that God was going to perform a miracle and shave off most of his sentence, at least only leaving a year or two. I'd already stuck with him through three, I could handle at least two more, but my mind couldn't wrap around another five. Another five years of making sure I bought clothes that were prison appropriate and wouldn't set off the metal detectors; five years of long drives to prisons in the middle of nowhere; five years of hearing, "You have 60 seconds remaining"; five years of, "Visitation is now over"; five years of, "Baby, when I come home, I promise ... "; five years of money on commissary and phone calls; five years of no dates and waking up alone; five years, five years, five years—five years to die a little more inside. I was trying to hold firm to the notion that I was doing God's will, but with each passing day, it became harder and harder for me to believe that. My love kept trying to convince me that we had to go through the tough times before the good times, and we just needed to hold on to our faith. Maybe I needed to pray more, and I tried to pray more, but as the days passed, the love I once felt was turning into resentment. I was emotionally, financially, and physically depleted. I began spending most of my days feeling depressed about the fact that the person I loved could not hold me when I had a rough day, or do the majority of the things that I felt a mate was to do. Every little thing that was once not a problem now began to bother me mercilessly. I started despising visitations where we sat like lab rats being watched by scientists for two-hour intervals. I began feeling resentful at the fact that bills were piling up due to all the money spent on lawyers, money on the phone, money on his books, money to travel to and from prison visits. That time should've been a happy time especially with the planning of our "wedding," but happy was far from what I felt.

I wanted an escape, and that door would be opened in the form of my pastor. I went to him to ask about his officiating our wedding ceremony at the prison. By this time I was in a state of, "I don't want to be married like this, but I don't want to disappoint my fiancé or God." However, in the conversation with my pastor, I found the ability to breathe again. I found the ability to see again. And so that day when I sat in the visitation room, it would be a visit like none of the others. It would be the day where I decided to choose me. I knew my fiancé loved me, I knew that with conviction. I loved him just as much, but something was still missing in the equation, and that was the fact that I didn't love me.

### *Words of Wisdom from Sam*

*Some may not believe in the prophetic word, but I am one who does and it is an important part of my story. One Friday night during a revival service, the woman of God told me that I was not going to have to worry about the men in my past because God had a man for me after His own heart, and I wouldn't worry because I* would know where he was. Roughly four months later, I was on my way to work, and the guy I spoke about above fell into my spirit. I asked around to see what had happened to him, but no one knew. I eventually learned that he was incarcerated, and instantly knew I wanted nothing to do with that. However, he fell into my spirit once again. This time I heeded what I felt and decided to send him a card. In the first letter he sent me, he told me that I was the only woman he ever loved. That was nice to hear, but I still wasn't completely sold on the idea of getting too close to someone who was incarcerated. However, as time progressed I found myself falling in love with him despite his situation. Remember the prophetic word I spoke about a few moments ago. I would use that prophetic word to seal the deal on why the guy above and I were "divinely" appointed for each other. She'd told me that "I would know where he was" and in the case of this guy I absolutely knew where he was 24/7 so this had to be the one even though it wasn't the most ideal situation.

After the first year of our relationship, I began to get very unhappy and confused with the thought of whether I heard God correctly. I was praying every day asking God for sign after sign to confirm this was right. I would think I had received a sign from God, but it would only give me temporary relief. Soon thereafter I'd be right back in a space of discontentment, convincing myself that I was like Jesus in the Garden of Gethsemane asking God to pass the cup from Him, but just like Christ I had to endure this situation. Do I believe God placed it in my spirit to reach out to him in his time of need? Yes. Was the purpose of my reaching out to him to become his "savior" and attach myself to a relationship like I had tried to do with every other man? No. I kept telling myself and everyone else who told me what I was doing was crazy, that they just didn't understand and I had to be longsuffering. I truly had myself convinced that God wanted me to go through this for

*His glory, but peace was always temporary. God was beginning to take me to a place where I was seeing my worth, and I knew I deserved more than what this man could be to me at that time. Even knowing this and how I felt, there was still a part of me that didn't want to be disobedient to God and focus too much on my feelings if this was truly what He wanted me to endure. I knew the wedding at that time was not of God, but walking away completely still seemed uncertain.*

*At my best friend's wedding, I saw the same woman of God and was hoping to get her alone for a few moments to ask her for clarification about the original prophecy. Before I could even get a chance to ask her for clarity, she said to me, "You're next. You're going to meet him there, and it will be about ministry." Just like that, it was as though someone had ripped the wool right off of my eyes. When the woman of God referenced "there," I took away two interpretations: either I'd meet the man God had for me in South Carolina, or I'd meet him while living in South Carolina. Either way, the prophetic speaking canceled out the guy in prison because we met in North Carolina, and that is where he was. This prompted me to take a closer look at the original prophecy, and there was a key part that I missed. "You won't worry about men in your PAST." I'd neglected that one small word. The guy was a man from my PAST, he was never the person the woman of God spoke to me about, but I had made him so.*

*If you are a Christian, and believe in prophetic words and have received them for your life, I pray that you are also seeking God to ensure that the word given to you is indeed for you, and not misinterpreted by you. I believe this can only truly be done by fostering a strong relationship with the Lord where you can hear His voice definitively. Otherwise, you will do as I did. I believe prophetic words should come as a confirmation to you and when* it is manifested in the natural, should bring a level of peace that surpasses all understanding, and not cause doublemindedness. True prophetic words should line up with the Word of God, and in my case, the Word of God speaks specifically about the role a husband should play in the marriage — my mate was limited in his capacity to act in that role.

If you are not spiritual and wanted to look at this situation from a non-spiritual standpoint, you can still see how it was my brokenness and lack of self-worth that kept me in that situation for three years. I don't condemn any woman who chooses to be with someone who is incarcerated, but my personal belief is that as God's Daughters of Freedom, He would not ever want us in situations where we are in bondage, and being with a man who is incarcerated is a form of bondage. My ex was safe for me. I knew he loved me and needed me, and in my brokenness that made me feel whole. I encourage you to give yourself the option to see who he is and would be once he was released from prison. I spent so much of my time living in the "potential." The potential of who we could be once he was released, and how everything would be okay once he came home. Many times in my dating life my cousin would tell me not to be with someone based on potential. When you choose to be with someone it should be based on what their current reality is, and if things changed that would simply be icing on the cake. When you choose to be with someone based on their potential, you run the risk of being disappointed in the event that they don't turn into the person you thought they could "potentially" become.

I struggled, I mean really, really struggled, with walking away from this situation. He wasn't a bad person, in fact, he is probably one of the sweetest men I've ever had the opportunity to encounter and words cannot express my sorrow for the pain I caused him. Even though the love was still there, my staying around *became more of obligation because I felt like it was my fault for letting it get as far as it did. I couldn't bear the thought of what would happen to him if I left. How could I break that kind of news to him when he was already in a destitute situation where I'd been his "light" in darkness? Early on he would tell me time and again to leave if I didn't think I could handle the situation, but being the "fixer" that I always was, I stayed. God has called us to aid people, not take His place by trying to be their savior. Sometimes three of the hardest things to do is let go, let God, and choose you.*

*Allow me to also share from this part of my story the fact that many times we can get caught up in situations that really aren't meant for us simply because the person is nice. What I know in my life right now is that nice is not enough. We can meet someone who is nice and they totally are on a different trajectory that we are as far as destiny is concerned, and I believe marriages should be destiny partnerships. Second Corinthians 6:14 talks specifically about not being unequally yoked. A yoke is a wooden bar that joins two oxen to each other and to the burden they pull. If the two oxen are of different characteristics (one strong, one weak, one short one tall), it makes pulling the load much more challenging. In the context of this situation in my story, we were very much unequally yoked in the current circumstance. His incarceration had placed an unfair burden on me where I felt like the "stronger ox" being forced to carry the most weight, attempting to take care of me and him while keeping my sanity. This was not the will of God for my life. The issue of being unequally yoked is so important I will touch on it again in the chapter on "Waiting on the Lord."*

*One final thing I want to glean from this part of my story is that something happening seamlessly is not always God's way of saying "yes" or "go." Although this can be true in some instances, I need to caution that it can also be untrue. I was slated to marry the guy who was incarcerated. We both completed the application per prison protocol. Now during this time I'd met a friend who was going through the process of trying to get approved to marry her boyfriend who was incarcerated, but she was having no luck getting the application approved or reaching anyone in administration to answer her questions on the application process. She began to think perhaps it wasn't meant to be. In my situation, I had no problems whatsoever reaching someone in administration. In fact, they were super helpful answering all my questions about the process. I was told that once the application was received it took 4-6 weeks for approval. I heard back about our application being approved in less than two weeks. This had to be right! It was too "seamless" not to be. Then one day, God sent an intervention by way of my pastor. Sometimes we can truly be on a path for derailment and God will attempt to block things that He knows is not the path we need to take. It is up to us whether we take heed to what God is trying to stop.*

## CHAPTER 10

# NEW ADDRESS, SAME MESS

I read a powerful statement once that said ships are safe in the harbor, but that's not what ships are built for. I'd add to that and say ships are meant to sail. I believe that life truly begins on the other side of our comfort zones. In 2013, I took the most courageous step of my life at that time. I moved to another state, ALONE—no friends, no family, no kids, husband, boyfriend, NOBODY—just me and God. I'd never lived anywhere besides North Carolina so there was a lot of excitement and anxiety about relocating. At the onset of my move, it seemed as though everything was falling into place seamlessly—this was a good seamless. Yes, I was enjoying my new surroundings, but what I had not accounted for was the cost of no longer being close to family and friends. My apartment which was supposed to be my safe haven had become a place I dreaded going because I felt so alone. I could not understand why God would have called me to this place to desert me. One evening in my despair I heard God tell me, "I isolated you, so I could elevate you," but I wasn't able to receive this. All I could dwell on was how alone I felt. I'd grown so much spiritually in the past three years, but it seemed as though I could not recall any of that and the enemy was ready to place another "lie limb" on the "tree of lies" in my life, attempting to take me back to a place that I thought was no longer me. After the move, I wasn't really meeting anyone so my friend suggested that I try some online dating just to meet new people in the area. I had some not so great experiences with online dating in the past, but I figured perhaps things were different in the online dating world at that time.

I met several guys, some nice, some not so nice, and most situations just fizzled out before they ever got started. I was prepared to give up on the entire online dating thing when I met what appeared to be a really nice guy. We began exchanging messages through the site and engaging in phone conversations soon after. One thing I knew with conviction that I wanted at that point in life was a man who was saved. I was elated when he told me that he was. In my mind, I began to think the situation would be very promising. I was so excited for our first date, but a red flag immediately went up the first moment I ever saw him. I was sitting outside the restaurant waiting for him to arrive, and as he walked up to the front door, I realized he was talking on his cell phone. In my mind surely he'd end his conversation with whomever he was speaking with, but he did not. In fact, he kept the conversation going for at least another couple of minutes as though I wasn't sitting there at all. I couldn't understand how that was a good first impression, but like with most red flags concerning men in my life, I brushed it aside. The date ended up going really well and we seem to have enjoyed each other's company with the promise of there being other dates, which there were. We'd become so comfortable with each other, that we'd began a ritual of dinner over movies at my apartment. I was "happy." He seemed to be genuinely interested and

I thought this was definitely going to turn into more than a friendship. Although there was a definite attraction to each other, we hadn't had sex which made me feel even better as I wanted to hold on to my vow of celibacy—the one I gained from being in a 3-year relationship with a guy who was incarcerated.

The tide turned the night we laid in my bed "playing around" after two bottles of wine. I hadn't had a problem with my celibacy up until that point. My flesh craved him and what's unfortunate is that it wasn't truly my commitment to Christ that kept me from crossing the sexual boundary, it was the fact that he wasn't aware of my deep dark secret. My history had proved to me that offering up such sensitive information that involved the words "I have" and "herpes" always changed things, and I didn't know if I was ready to give up my only friend just yet. However, that night as we lay across my bed, the wine had given me liquid courage and I found the words "me" and "herpes" rolling off of my lips. After my announcement I tried to use the streetlight pouring through the window to see the expression on his face, hoping it wasn't one of disgust. Ironically, his words to me were, "I've been in this type of situation before," and I felt relief wash over me and an increased desire to want him more. At that moment, the only thing that mattered to me was thanking him for not heading for the hills. As I'm sure you've gathered by now, my "thank you's" involved letting him inside of me. After our initial encounter, we decided that we needed to have a "sober" redo which would lead to many more, and in my mind a relationship was right around the corner, but he had other ideas. He eventually told me words that were very familiar to me and they go something like this: "I'm not looking for anything serious." I had come to learn through trial and error that when a man said that, he meant it.

For months, he and I would keep up this routine, and on the surface, if you looked closely at what we were doing there was a resemblance to a relationship, but a resemblance of something is not the same as it actually being that. I'd keep telling myself I was okay with what we were, knowing I desired more. I'd have lapses of time where I knew I deserved better and would stop talking to him only to call him back saying I was wrong and I was really okay with us being friends, knowing I was not. Then the real trouble happened—I fell in love with him. You're probably wondering why that is trouble because love is a beautiful entity. It's trouble when the love is not reciprocated. This had nothing to do with any false hope given on his end because he'd already made it clear what he wanted, but the more he said no, the more my heart said yes. For him each stroke between my thighs was just part of the journey to get him to ecstasy after which he could wash his hands, put on his clothes, and look right past the emptiness left behind my eyes as he closed the front door. It was an emptiness that screamed, "Stay! Let me lay my head on your chest, and be lulled to sleep by the sound of your heartbeat." Why couldn't I make it just sex, instead of having each climax tighten the strings of my heart? Why was the time leading up to every moment spent with him filled with so much anticipation like a child unable to sleep on Christmas Eve? I begged, cried, and pleaded with my heart, "Don't do this to me," but it turned a deaf ear to my pleas as if we were complete strangers. I was a completely emotional train wreck over this guy. The ironic part about it was that months prior to this point I found myself sobbing relentlessly after his leaving and my not wanting him to go. In that moment, I heard the Holy Spirit clear as day say to me, "He's not the one," but I wanted him to be and he was the only thing I felt I had to hold onto in such a lonely place. I found myself relapsing to a place I once knew, a place I felt with conviction that God had delivered me from … or had He?

## *Words of Wisdom by Sam*

Isolation is not one of those words that necessarily holds positive context. When you hear the word isolation one might think of loneliness, but in some cases isolation is necessary. In my case, God had isolated me for a reason, but the enemy had my mind so wrapped around how alone I felt, I could not focus on what God's purpose for my isolation was. For me, God's isolation had two purposes: (1) to grow my relationship with Him, and (2) to further His purpose through me. The situation that I was in with the guy who was incarcerated grew my relationship with Christ like never before. In moving to South Carolina God wanted to take me to another level, and in doing that He had to grow me to another level. Growing pains are real and can be applied to various parts of life. We cannot grow in anything without being stretched. I told the Lord that I wanted Him to have His way in my life, and in doing so He needed to grow me. Sometimes it is hard for God to grow us the way He wants to when we are in comfortable surroundings. Sometimes He will take us to a place where we must fully trust, lean on, and rely on Him. I also believe that it's in our isolation where we can hear from God the best if we want to. I have to place emphasis on the "want to," because God is a true gentleman and will never force Himself on us. God had placed me in the perfect position to hear from Him, but as I said above I was too fixated on feeling "alone."

But one day that changed. Instead of focusing on how sad or lonely I felt not really knowing anyone or having family close by, I began to pick up the Word of God a little more, spending more time in meditation and prayer, allowing God to love on me as He wanted to. I realized that God had isolated me to further His purpose through me. I've known from childhood that God had gifted me with the art of writing and in adulthood, He has exposed to me that He will use the gift He has given me for His glory. For *many years, God had placed it on my heart to write a book, but I struggled with the topic and actually taking the time to sit down and write. When I moved to South Carolina, I didn't have as many social connections which meant more time alone which equated to time that I could spend working on the book that God put in me to encourage His Daughters of Promise. It has taken almost two years for me to finally get to a place of understanding of what God is doing. Now let's be clear as I don't want anyone to be disillusioned. After realizing the purpose for my isolation, the enemy still tried me and continues to try me by attempting to attack my mind with ill thoughts about my isolation even as I write this book. But the beauty is that I know the reasoning so his attacks are very short-lived. My beloved sister, if you are going through a period of isolation in your life, I encourage you to truly spend some time seeking the Lord on what the reasoning behind the isolation is, as there is a reason and it has nothing to do with whatever lies the enemy has tried to plant in your mind. We must be mindful that above all else, we were created to fulfill the Will of God.*

## CHAPTER 11

# FALSE POSITIVE

I can remember being curled up on my bedroom floor praying to God to just help me get through the moment. The pain I was experiencing was almost too much to bear. All that kept playing in my head like a broken record were his words, "I thought this was what I wanted, but I was wrong." It couldn't be so. We were in love—I was betrothed to him, he said so himself. I'd even done everything right this time, not rushing into anything, following his lead. It had to have been a nightmare. God loved me and He would never have played such a cruel joke on me. Our first date was one to remember—Valentine's Day to be exact. Our first meeting was actually going to be a blind date. I wasn't sure how I felt about that, but he came highly recommended so I figured I'd be opened minded. For the first part of our date, I was to meet him for dinner. I was overwhelmingly surprised to realize we were eating at a Brazilian Steakhouse (in case you've never been there, the food's awesome and is at least $50 a person). When I opened the restaurant door, he stood there with a dozen long-stemmed red roses. He had me at hello (hee hee). Dinner turned into roller skating which turned into long conversations over Starbucks coffee late into the night. I felt good about him, and I'd say he did as well serenading me with Anthony Hamilton's "The Point of it All."

He seemed to be everything I'd prayed for and most importantly a man of God. Not only was he handsome, kind, successful, and a true gentleman, but I didn't have to water down my love for Christ because he, too, seemed very much in love with Him. We gravitated to each other so quickly it scared me. Oh, I was over the moon happy, so glad that God had sent me my Boaz. I'd watch him usher in the Holy Spirit through praise and worship at his church and my heart would just be overwhelmed with my gift from God. God had answered my prayer and gave me the evidence I needed to show the world, especially the women I was seeking to empower, that He truly was a restorer of all things. Even though we'd only known each other a short time, we began making plans for our future. It really was all happening so fast, but God created the world in six days, surely He did not need to take years to send me my mate.

Yes, I knew this was it, but there in the midst of my delight, something began to change. I started to notice him becoming more and more emotionally detached. My past had taught me to overanalyze everything, and because I wanted everything to be different with this guy, I just overlooked certain things—certain things like something doesn't feel right. There came a point when I realized that our mutually great desire to spend time with each other was turning into indifference on his part with his citing that he liked being alone. This seemed a bit oxymoronic considering the conversations about how we both greatly longed for godly companionship. I had to ask if we were okay. He assured me that we were, telling me all the right things to ease my unsettledness, but it would only be temporary. The feeling of something being wrong would come again and we'd have another conversation, only this time he wouldn't be assuring me everything was fine. This time he would be telling me how he wasn't really comfortable with the fact that I'd received all of these spiritual confirmations about him, but he had yet to receive anything in the spiritual about me but felt he should have. I suppose I could not argue with that. He expressed concerns about his fears of being unable to remain faithful to me due to my desire to lose weight and his attraction was to plus-sized women. He felt the woman for him would be what he liked with no plans to change like I was, so this added to his uncertainty about me. I finally had to ask him was he saying that we were done and he would go on to tell me that he thought this relationship was what he wanted, but he was wrong. Those words fell on my ears like someone scraping their fingernails against a blackboard. What was he possibly talking about? He was the one! The one God created for me! It was confirmed! I didn't get it wrong this time, I didn't! How he could he be flipping the script? He said he loved me and wanted me to be with him and I was amazing! These are all things I wanted to scream through the phone, but instead, I told him I understood and wasn't upset. But I didn't understand and I was upset. Upset and heartbroken ... again.

### *Words of Wisdom from Sam*

*Here is where I need to bring up the topic around discerning the voice of God, and will actually devote a chapter to this topic later in the book. For the second time in my life, I'd taken a prophetic word and applied it as I wanted. I'm a believer in prophetic utterances, but also a believer that what is spoken into your life should confirm what you already know or God should also give that word directly to you. I applied the prophecy to this situation because I knew the deliverer was a mighty worker for the*

*Lord, and I truly didn't feel adequate enough to actually hear from the Lord myself. I'd realize later that I could, I just didn't know it. As good as I felt things were with me and the guy, there was still an uneasiness and questions of, "are we okay." Those feelings were not just coincidental they were promptings from the Holy Spirit, saying, "Hey, hey, this isn't it." As Daughters of Freedom, we must learn the imperativeness of being able to discern God's voice for ourselves.*

But what I truly love about God is that He is so merciful and full of grace, He will protect us by blocking things that we can't even see coming. I'm reminded of a photo I saw on social media where a woman was just walking down the street and all around her angels were slaying things that she couldn't even see trying to attack her. In this situation, I was preparing to uproot my life and move to a new city for a man that God never intended to be for me. Because I wasn't able to discern His voice saying, "STOP," he changed the guy's heart. If I may, allow me to offer another reason I believe God changed the guy's heart. I was supposed to be fulfilling an assignment—writing this book. At the time when we dated, I was working the traditional 9-5 job, and the only free time I had was in the evenings, but was I writing in that free time? No. I was on the phone with my new boyfriend until the wee hours of the morning. This may seem radical, but I believe God will take things away from us if He sees it will threaten what He calls us to do. In my case, God knew I didn't have the discipline to do both at that time—we can't fool God! I'm sure God knew losing this guy would hurt me, and even though I knew He was concerned with my pain, He was also concerned with my destiny.

One final thing I'd like to pull from this part of my story is around sex and the Christian. I will delve into the topic a bit more in the chapter on waiting on the Lord, but I need to touch on it here *just a bit. Even in the relationship that I felt God put together, we seemed to be on one accord in terms of our walk with Christ, but the physical aspect was a bit of an issue. I went into the situation truly radical, wanting to do things completely different and that included not even kissing to keep at bay the sexual desires that are natural. I could tell this was a strain in our relationship and I found myself compromising in the area of oral sex. I have to be brutally honest with this to emphasize how the enemy will try to trick you into thinking the only sexual act that matters is intercourse and it's okay because "we love each other." Sometimes as Christians, we want to flirt around with the idea that what we're doing is okay as long as we're not having sex, but that is untrue. If you are a single woman who is striving to live for Christ and wonder if you've met the godly man for you, ask yourself, "Does he ask me to compromise **any** of my values especially as it relates to pleasing God?" If this answer is anything but "no," please understand that your godly man will never ask you to compromise what you stand for in Christ especially if he is supposed to be striving to stand for the same thing. A godly man will never encourage you to participate in something that the Word of God specifically speaks against. Now don't get me wrong, he could be the one but perhaps there are still some kinks that God needs to work out in him. Remember He is a jealous God, and He would never desire to see you with a person who would intentionally try to persuade you away from what's pleasing to Him. If your vow to God or just your desire is to not have sex until marriage, the man for you will honor that vow and respect it because he respects you. If you have to compromise your body to keep him, he is not the one, point ... blank ... and the period.*

# CHAPTER 12

# REBOUND

"We're just not compatible," was the answer I heard to my question, "Why can't we be together?" The irony of the situation at that moment was that this conversation was held as we both lay naked in my bed. Perhaps it was the weed we smoked earlier that had me confused, but my brain could not make sense of how we could sleep together, having slept together for close to two years off and on, yet not be compatible. I had rebounded back to a past bad decision. My heart was so very broken after it didn't work out with the guy I thought was "the one," and to be honest I was a bit upset with God as well. I couldn't understand why He hadn't intervened before I got hurt. I decided to call back upon the one consistent "friend" I had made using the one thing that had bonded us for more than a year – sex. Throwing caution to the wind we fell back into each other's bed as though we'd never stopped. The recommitment I'd made to God with my ex about keeping my body pure until marriage had gone completely out the window. Just like that, I'd found myself doing all the things I'd always done with him—all things I knew were not pleasing to God—drinking, smoking, sex. It was almost as if I were angry with God for "dangling the carrot" with my Boaz who turned out to be a fraud, and because of this, I didn't really know if there was a point to living holy. Things seemed to go well with my "friend with benefits" and I after picking up our old routine. We were speaking daily again, hanging out at each other's houses, working out together— yes things seemed really good, that is if you consider good, true dysfunction. Perhaps I should give you a bit more context into our story.

When I decided to make the decision to move from Spartanburg to the next city over, this decision was based on the fact that I'd heard so many great things about the larger city and loved it the times I'd been there. But the larger reason was because I wanted to live with my "friend with benefits" rebound guy. I needed him or so I thought. He was currently living with family and looking for a roommate situation so we both thought it could be a win-win. I must admit I went into the situation with some ulterior motives. Surely, if we lived together and I played the role of "wife," he would see how valuable I was to his life and wouldn't be able to live without me. I'd been vetting different properties with my "friend with benefits" because he was a native of the city. I came across one particular property and he informed me that he was just thinking how he would love to live in that area since it was very close to his job. When I went to visit the property, I instantly fell in love. I put my application in on the spot, and less than an hour later the property management company was calling me to tell me that I was approved. This had to be God's "yes" I should move. The process was too "seamless" for it to be anything else. So I moved.

It wasn't long before I'd realize God's silence was not a yes, and once again in my life "seamless" did not equate to "go." The day my FWB (friend with benefits) came to help me move boxes and check out his new room, my opinion of what I thought the situation would turn into started to change. I can remember the two of us standing at the top of the staircase looking at our adjacent bedrooms and him saying, "Ugh you're going to be able to hear everything." I wasn't sure what that comment meant, but the embarrassed look he had on his face made me think he was referring to my being able to hear when he had other women over. I felt a bit saddened and realized my "dream plan" may not go as I originally thought. Things seemed to be good with us and we were still on target to have him move in the first of the year, which at that time was only a couple of months away. After one of our "FWB episodes," I felt so sad after he left. I truly felt like he was able to just "make love" to me like he loved me, yet get up, put on his clothes, and walk out the door like I was some cheap thrill. I decided to write about that incident and share it with him thinking it would tug on his heart strings and make him see the error of his ways. It did not. What it did do was prompt him to tell me that it was no longer a good idea for us to be roommates. I could not understand. A part of me was upset because he'd changed his mind after I moved, but the larger part of me was upset because my plan to try and make him want to be with me was now done.

A couple of months later I realized that the move had put me in a horrible financial position, much worse than when I was living in Spartanburg. I'd taken out a loan to pay for the deposit which left me with a $200 monthly bill I hadn't had before. I doubled the amount of gas I'd spend a month to get to work due to my now much longer commute. All of my utility bills increased greatly. I'd maxed out my credit cards trying to pay bills. I became a regular at the Payday Loan and Cash Advance places. I began "robbing Peter to pay Paul." Bills began piling up. Disconnection notices began pouring in. I was on the phone every month with the bank setting up arrangements for them not to repossess my car. I was having to reach out to my church to seek assistance for utility bills. I was having to go to local food pantries to get food because every cent was accounted for with none remaining for grocery. I was working two jobs as long as I physically could to try and stay afloat. I'd fallen into a slight depression as I watched the credit score I'd worked so hard to get back on track from my college years, fall three hundred points in less than a year. I began feeling angry as I watched my FWB seem to thrive financially, while I struggled to keep from drowning. I was angry with God because I thought the "seamless" process meant yes, and I was following His lead. However, the reality is I'd fallen into the trap of the enemy yet again, all because I craved to be loved by a person who had made it clear from the beginning that he was not interested in loving me in any way, shape, form, or fashion. Yet once again there I lay in my bed with a man who wined and dined other women while I struggled to eat, and took trips with other women in public, while he entered my body in secret in a house I was close to losing because I loved him and hated me. Was this life?

### *Words of Wisdom from Sam*

*The first piece of wisdom I'd like re-emphasize is not to confuse the ease of things happening with that being God's way of saying, "This is what I want you to do." Everything that happens effortlessly is not always of God (remember my example earlier in the book), that's why it is so important to have a strong relationship with Him that would make it easier to discern His voice. In my story, by no means was it God's will for me to move to another city especially to be roommates with another man. We may be able to fool ourselves, but we cannot fool God. He would never suggest I do that knowing the guy and I were already living in sin separately, how much easier would it be to further that agenda living under* the same roof? My choice to move was what I wanted to do, and I asked God to bless it. He doesn't operate that way. The safest place on earth is in the Will of God. God knows the plan for our life and when we take matters into our own hands and deviate from the plan, things get messy. The beauty about having a loving, heavenly Father is that He is full of grace and mercy and will help us get back on track if we so desire.

The second piece of wisdom I'd like to pull out is around identifying people who can act as illusions and being able to discern the difference between assets and liabilities in your life. When I checked the Thesaurus on other words for illusion, I found words like trickery and deception. When we think about people in our lives who are an illusion of something, it can feel like we are being tricked or deceived. Daughters of Freedom understand their self-worth so much, that they are able to see people for who they really are. For example, if their actions aren't lining up with who they proclaim to be, they are simply an illusion, and illusions are usually liabilities and not assets. With this guy, he told me he was saved. That was simply an illusion because nothing about his actions lined up with a man following Christ. We need to be careful not to swoon over a man just because they say they are saved. In this case, we really need to look for action and not just word.

When we think about people in our lives, I like to think of two categories: assets and liabilities. An asset *is defined as a useful or valuable thing, person, or quality.* Synonyms for the word asset include benefit, advantage, *and* blessing. One definition by Merriam-Webster of liability *is someone or something that causes problems.* [2] Synonyms for liability include hindrance *or* burden. One

---

2   Merriam-Webster. Accessed February 28, 2016. http://www.merriam-webster.com/dictionary/liability.

*tricky thing to note about assets and liabilities is that if a person does not know their self-worth they can easily confuse a liability with an asset because when you have a low self-worth, something that is likely not good for you, can look good simply because you don't think you deserve better.*

People who are assets in your life add value in some form. They usually own characteristics that include being responsible, respectable, trustworthy, selfless, and consistent just to name a few. A person who is an asset to your life will always want to see you be the very best version of yourself, even if it means telling you the truth in love. A quick question to ask yourself when wondering if someone is an asset to your life is if they were no longer around, would my life be better or worse? Now note again that this question can only be answered truthfully if you have a full awareness of who you are and what you deserve. Otherwise, your answer could be misguided. People who are liabilities to your life take away value in some form. They usually own characteristics that include those that are directly opposite of a person who is an asset – irresponsible, disrespectful, not trustworthy, selfish, and inconsistent, just to name a few. Ask yourself the same question from above to help you identify if people in your life are liabilities or not.

The third piece of Wisdom I'd like to pull from this story is around soul ties. With the guy in this story, for close to two years we would be on this rollercoaster of me saying, "I deserve better," but falling right back into bed with him. I'd keep having moments of, "I've had enough," then find myself trying to maneuver my way back into his life. This up and down, back and forth behavior happened so much, that he got tired of excusing my "roller coaster" behavior and quite frankly thought I was crazy. As "crazy" as it seemed, having him not "take me back" couldn't be an option, I needed him in my life. I would find myself sending text after text *saying how apologetic I was for taking him through so much and I "deserved" for him to treat me so coldly after all I'd taken him through.*

*One evening after a slew of "apology" texts, I sat on my couch feeling so very sad and confused. Yearning for him so greatly was insane, and the other part of my mind knew this! This guy had not treated me as I deserved, and I knew the lifestyle I was living was not pleasing to God, yet I still wanted everything to do with him. I could not understand this. Why was this so? This is when the Holy Spirit dropped into my spirit the term "soul tie." I'd heard this phrase spoken before but wasn't knowledgeable about what a soul tie actually was. I decided I needed to learn more about soul ties and so began my quest for more knowledge. The verdict: I was indeed tied to this man or his spirit rather, hence why it was so challenging to let him go even when I absolutely knew I should.*

*From my research, I found that a* soul tie *is defined as "a spiritual connection between two people who have been physically intimate with each other or who have had an intense emotional or spiritual association or relationship."*[3] *A soul tie can be either a good thing or a bad thing. The Bible doesn't mention the term soul tie specifically, but it does reference the description of a soul tie as it relates to marriage discussed in Matthew 19:5, or the description of the close friendship between David and Jonathan in 1 Samuel 18:1. The soul ties found in those passages of scriptures are positive ones, bringing about results that can enhance the life of another person.*

*However, in my case, when I speak of a soul tie, I'm not referencing one that has a positive impact, I'm referencing the kind that has the potential to steal, kill, and destroy, and we know*

---

3   Tim Stewart. "Soul Ties (and Break Soul Ties)." Dictionary of Christianese. 2014. Accessed March 22, 2016. http://www.dictionaryofchristianese.com/soul-ties/.

*whose motive that is—the devil. When a person comes in contact with a negative soul tie, this presents a window of opportunity for demonic forces to enter into the person's life and wreak havoc. Some believe that sex is just sex, nothing more nothing less, but that is a dangerous misconception. Women are more inclined to be deeply affected by soul ties because during the act of sex we are on the receiving end. Scripture says that the Holy Spirit resides inside of us. When we have sex, the man also physically enters the inside of us transferring his spirit to us. When you have the Holy Spirit living on the inside of you and a spirit that is not like the Holy Spirit also gets deposited inside of you, there becomes a war between the two, and they cannot coexist. The Holy Spirit is the One telling us that the way we are living is not right, but the demonic spirit also prompts us to continue the life we're living.*

*After realizing what was ailing me, I emailed my pastor from back home and asked him how did I rid myself of this soul tie, how did I give the boot to the spirit inside of me that was not good? His prescription to me was to flex the Holy Spirit who resides on the inside of me because light will always drive out darkness. He quoted one of my favorite Scriptures, I John 4:4 which says, "...because the one who is in you is greater than the one who is in the world." This meant that the Holy Spirit could override the demonic spirit that was plaguing me, I just needed to "flex" my spirit. Before being able to flex your spirit, you first must be able to acknowledge that you are experiencing the effects of a soul tie, and not just the break-up blues—it's deeper than that. Then you must repent and re-anchor your soul in the Lord. The night I had an awareness of my own soul tie, I lay before the Lord asking God to deliver me, and when He did, to also help me stay free.*

*One of my favorite sermons is Juanita Bynum's "No More Sheets." I don't know if she says the words soul tie verbatim, but she does state the fact that many women who have participated in pre-marital sex desire marriage not realizing they have been married multiple times over with other partners, yet there was no divorce. The act of consummation or sex was designed for marriage because it binds two people in the spiritual realm. When we have pre-marital sex over and over we become one with multiple people, yet never separate from them even after a breakup occurs. Have you ever found yourself wondering why you couldn't seem to move on from someone who wasn't good for you, or still thought of an ex long after the relationship ended? The verdict is that there is likely still a soul tie that has not been severed, and must be for you to be free. Allow me to leave you with one final thought around soul ties: a soul tie is the knitting together of two souls that can either bring tremendous blessings in a godly relationship or tremendous destruction when made with the wrong people—please choose wisely.*

*The final piece of wisdom I'd like to share from this story is simply the fact that people will do what you allow. With this guy, there is one thing that I must give him credit for above all the other men I've had in my life: he was honest and stayed consistent with the fact that he was not interested in a romantic relationship with me. As women, we rarely take men at face value when they tell us something upfront like that. We often have the mindset that we can change their minds or prove to them that they need us in their life. We think if we play the role of "significant other," this will change their mind about not wanting a "significant other." With this guy we were doing things that couples would do: talking on the phone daily and spending consistent time together, so in my mind that equated to us moving closer to a relationship, but in his mind, the "I don't want anything serious" meter had not moved in my favor. Ladies, men can enjoy your company and the benefits of acting like a couple without desiring to actually be a couple. This is where accountability comes in along with the notion of people doing what we allow. For this guy, I'd broken a 3-year vow of celibacy, spent two years giving my body to him, lost almost everything I had to be with him, but as angry as I wanted to be with him about all of that, the only person I could truly be upset with was me. How could I be angry with something I approved to happen when I knew the facts?*

*If you know that you desire a relationship, and the guy is telling you that he is not looking for a relationship, that is when the ball is placed back in your court and you have to make the decision to stick around or keep it moving. If you stick around hoping that he will change his mind, you are living in the realm of potential, and as I discussed earlier that is a dangerous place to live. You cannot get mad at the guy for allowing you to play the part you chose to play when you were informed from the beginning. That's like you asking someone to hold some money for you and they tell you upfront they are going to spend it. If you give it to them anyway, and they spend it, can you be angry with that person? No. You had the facts but chose to take the unwise path anyway, and for that there are consequences. We'll talk more about accountability in a later chapter.*

# PART 2

# FREEDOM

CHAPTER 13

# CHANGING TIDE

This is the part of my story that makes me the most excited to share as it's the part where the rubber finally met the road. After things just completely down-spiraled with my FWB (friend with benefits) and it seemed I'd expended all of my "options" for physical love, I realized I needed to actively find a way to get to the bottom of my decade-long search for love and feeling good enough. I truly, *truly* was tired. This part of my story reminds of Jesus and the Samaritan woman at the well. Jesus told her that if she drunk from the water in the well she'd thirst again, but if she drunk from Him—the living water—she'd thirst no more. For my entire life, I kept drinking from the well that contained water that always left me thirsty, and I needed to get serious about getting in tune with the One who would give me living water where I would thirst no more. I had done the dance with so many different men of different ages and caliber, yet the outcome always ended the same. I'd listened to enough women's empowerment messages to know that I was more than enough and any man should be happy to have me in his life, but why weren't they happy to have me in their life? I mean, come on, I was the common denominator in all of the equations so it had to be me. And it was me!

One day during one of my lowest points, a friend invited me to attend her church. I need to put a pin here to tell you about how we met. She and I met through a mutual friend that was a colleague to both of us many years apart. She worked with her in Philadelphia, I worked with her years later in North Carolina. We both ended up in South Carolina and were in similar places in our lives. That's not a coincidence, that's God—He is true provision. He will orchestrate things so beautifully, even as a writer I can't do it justice. The Sunday that she invited me to church, I can recall looking over the program and noticing that one of the services they offered was lay counseling. I wasn't sure if this service would be available to me since I wasn't a member, and I wasn't completely comfortable with counseling, but I knew I was going through one of the roughest patches of my life and I needed help. I came to learn that the counseling was free and offered to anyone interested, so every Tuesday at 6:00 PM I began having a standing appointment with a woman whose presence in my life changed my life. My spirit was so downtrodden during our first session, but a few sessions in, I realized that her allowing me a space to be vocally free made me feel lighter. Meeting with her gave me a judgment free zone where I could verbalize all the bad decisions I'd made that had placed me in a life of bondage.

As our sessions progressed, all I wanted to do was talk about the men who had hurt me to my core, but I began to notice that subtly in our conversations she would begin to ask me questions about my father and his passing. I'd never been uncomfortable talking about my father's passing, but I realized that is because I never talked about it for an extended period of time. During every prolonged conversation we would have about my father's passing, I'd notice an uncomfortable tightness in my chest. I was smiling on the outside, but trying to keep my composure on the inside. This made me think back to other incidences where I'd talk to people about losing my father. I could speak about the incident abstractly, but never in-depth. One particular session, my counselor said to me, "Take me back there. I want to know how you really felt." I'd talked about his death on various occasions, but no one had ever asked me how I "felt" about his death, at least not that I can remember. Everyone would always ask if I was okay, which of course my response was "Yes," because I was okay in the sense of still breathing, but what I "felt" was indescribable hurt. Hurt that would be buried deeply for more than a decade. Hurt that left a hole in my heart. For fourteen years, I'd attempted to self-medicate myself to numb the pain. The loss of my father left me feeling abandoned. I used men to try and fill the void he left, and as you've read in previous chapters, I was doing any and everything to keep them from abandoning me like I felt he did.

But the root was deeper than just my father's passing. Through recommendations, I began participating in Theophostic Prayer and Celebrate Recovery. Celebrate Recovery is a Christ-Centered Recovery program that uses a 12-step process to help you find healing in your life. Theophostic Prayer is a form of ministry designed to help wounded people get to the root of their deep-rooted emotional issues. Through these two initiatives I began learning that the enemy had planted the seed of lies way before my father passed; his passing simply added gasoline to the fire. I know some of you who are likely reading this book have experienced some type of hurt in your life that you never fully dealt with, but rather buried it deep inside. My beloved sister, allow me to stress to you the importance of allowing God to expose your hurts *and* heal you. When we were birthed into this earth, God had a purpose for our lives. Situations may have happened to make you think you have no real purpose, but the devil is a liar! Regardless of what you've gone through, if you have breath in your body God still wants to fulfill that purpose. But in order for that to happen, you must be made whole. In order to be completely made whole, we have to be able to trust God with our pain. We must learn how to be vulnerable and say to him, "Daddy, I don't want to carry this burden any longer; heal me!" Please do not think this will be an overnight process, because it will not. But it will be a process that is worth it.

# CHAPTER 14

# FUNCTIONALLY BROKEN

This may sound ironic, but I consider myself to be a blessed person with herpes. For those of you not familiar with the herpes virus, there are two types: oral and genital. I contracted Genital Herpes. In the nine years since I contracted the disease, I've only experienced one outbreak— that is almost unheard of. You see in my case, it wasn't the physical aspect of having herpes that affected my life, it was the emotional aspect. Because I've been truly blessed to not suffer from outbreaks, physically I feel like any other person, but because I'm still a carrier of the virus, I feel it necessary to share the information so my partner has the right to make an informed decision—that is where my suffering came in. My suffering has been emotional, not physical. We live in a society that places much stigma on sexually transmitted diseases and the types of people that acquire them. Society paints a picture of those who have sexually transmitted diseases as being nasty or dirty, but that wasn't me. Yes, I was having unprotected sex, but that's not uncommon. I just happened to come across a person who had the disease as well. I won't bog you down with a bunch of statistical numbers, but 1 in 3 people have herpes. It's not uncommon at all. Regardless of the statistics or whether I had one outbreak or twenty, just knowing I was a carrier of the disease left me in a state of functional brokenness—this is a state not uncommon for most women.

My definition of functional brokenness is someone who looks like they have it all together on the outside and are able to fulfill day-to-day tasks with excellence but are completely emotionally unhealthy and dead on the inside. A person can be functionally broken for a variety of reasons that one way or another tie back to seeds the enemy planted: physical or sexual abuse as a child, being bullied in school, low self-esteem, loss of someone special in their life. I never fully grieved the loss of my father, rather placing Band-Aids over my wound. Once the Band-Aid became nasty from long wear, I'd simply change it, placing a fresh Band-Aid over the wound, but never allowing the wound to fully heal. Growing up I can remember having wounds and after a certain time my mother wouldn't bandage them up any longer, rather citing that they needed to be uncovered to heal completely. This is the same idea with functional brokenness. When I started going to counseling I began to see so much spiritual growth and began feeling God's restoration in so many areas, but God could not heal or restore that which I would not fully expose to Him. God is a gentleman. He does not force Himself on us or force us to turn things over to Him—that is why we have free will.

Here is a quick aside for my single sisters who feel they are ready for marriage but are still in the season of waiting. Perhaps there is some internal work that needs to be done. Scripture says that a man who finds a wife finds a GOOD thing (see Proverbs 18:22). It didn't say a man who finds a wife finds a functionally broken thing; it said a good thing, a healed thing, and a restored thing. As much as I wanted to "argue" with God that I was ready for Him to send my mate, He knew I was not. God knew that I was broken and that if He tried to send me a good man, I couldn't receive him because my self-worth was so low. As I've said before, we can't fool God. Allow me to talk to you now about the steps I utilized to shed my bondage and walk in freedom.

# CHAPTER 15

# GETTING TO THE ROOT OF WHAT AILS YOU

One of my favorite puns is, "Denial is not just a river." For most women, who like me, seemed to have lost their way or felt life has left them broken in some capacity, there is usually an underlying culprit. This culprit is usually a traumatic event that could have occurred either in childhood or adulthood. As discussed earlier, my first traumatic event happened in 6th grade. To be honest, when I started my quest to freedom, the Holy Spirit kept bringing back to my remembrance the 6th-grade incident, but I thought it too silly to really be part of my issue. Allow me to say to you, a tree grows from a seed, so nothing is ever too silly or insignificant to be considered the root of where your issues stem from. I'd go so far as to even say that is what the enemy wants you to believe so that you can just pluck what's seen above ground, but we all know anything can grow back if the roots aren't pulled. The passing of my father would simply put Miracle Grow on the seed the enemy planted.

About a year ago, I watched an episode of a show hosted by one of my favorite self-help experts, Iyanla Vanzant. The show was on "daddyless daughters." I'd never heard this term before and was intrigued to learn more. What I learned was that daddyless daughters are women whose fathers were not present in their lives, and this, in turn, had a great impact on them as a person, especially in the area of dating and relationships with men. Daddyless daughters can include women whose fathers were never present in their lives, women whose fathers were around for a while, but suddenly disappeared (my case), and fathers who had a physical presence in the home, but were not there for their daughters emotionally. As the episode progressed, I realized that I was indeed a daddyless daughter and could recognize the impact that losing my father had on my life. I've heard some controversy around women identifying themselves as daddyless daughters. Some have the viewpoint that accepting this type of label is negative and could make one feel inferior. However, I would disagree with that viewpoint. I don't see the label as being negative, nor does it make me feel inferior. What I believe is that identifying myself as a daddy-less daughter shows that I am ready to acknowledge and own my issue.

When I joined the Celebrate Recovery program, I noticed that the first thing we did in each session was to say our name and what we felt our issue was. I was very uncomfortable with this, further realizing it was just a form of acknowledgment. We have to be able to own what is ours, otherwise, we will only live in denial. Does identifying myself as a daddyless daughter mean I'd never be able to accomplish anything in life? Absolutely not! God has blessed me to accomplish much in my life, and I know plenty of women who could identify as daddyless daughters who have also been successful in their lives. However, this reminds me of the term I used in the previous chapter, "Functionally Broken." We can be the most successful woman in the world and still suffer from emotional issues as a result of not having a father figure in our lives. Like for me, this shows up most in our relationships with men. In order to get our boat out of the river of denial, we have to go back to the root. I will be completely honest in telling you that identifying the root will likely be uncomfortable as it's going to expose some old wounds and past hurts that have been deeply buried or you've never wanted to deal with.

> *In order to get our boat out of the river of denial, we have to go back to the root.*

When you do not deal with the root issue of your problem, you may have temporary results, but the issue will always rear its ugly head again. It's like putting a Band-Aid on a wound that needs stitches. It may work temporarily, but eventually, the Band-Aid will no longer be able to constrain the bleeding, and you will need to go to the hospital to get stitches.

    I used to be under the impression that deep rooted issues only needed to be addressed for single people. If you were in a committed relationship, you'd already won the "prize" so there was no need to change anything or deal with any issues you had, because it was obvious that your significant other loved you with your issues. However, I realized that deep rooted issues need to be exposed and acknowledged regardless. If you are a single person, exposing your issues will allow you to just be a healthier person emotionally, and if God blesses you to become part of a relationship, you will be the healthiest version of yourself. If you are currently in a relationship, exposing your issue will help your relationship in the long run because perhaps your issue has not yet shown up and therefore your mate does not know it exists. This could cause major strife later on down the road. As I said earlier, Band-Aids on severe wounds only last temporarily and eventually your issue will resurface.

When I decided that enough was enough, it became very clear that this was a process I would not be able to get through on my own, and I am so thankful that God placed amazing women in my life who could support me on my journey to freedom. The enemy has zero desire in seeing you free, so attempting to do so in isolation is a recipe for disaster. Why? Because the enemy uses isolation to prey heavily on your mind. When you've made up in your mind that you've had enough, you need to be praying for God to connect you with right places and people. My right place started in Christian lay counseling, which extended to Theophostic Prayer and joining Celebrate Recovery, all entities that have allowed me to release the chains in safe environments among women who were walking the journey with me. When you get sick and tired of being sick and tired and are ready to release your chains, you need women around you who can pray with you, encourage you, allow you to cry, or even make you laugh. As sisters in Christ, we are called to do life together, and that's why I'm so excited about ministry.

# CHAPTER 16

# ACCEPTANCE

It's great to have identified the root issue and acknowledged what has left us broken, but this means very little unless we are able to accept our issue. To me acceptance says, I've realized what my illness is and I won't be in a state of denial by acting as though the diagnosis doesn't exist; I just want to know how to be healed. Acceptance is the enemy of denial. Denial is the enemy's territory. He likes for us to stay in a state of denial about our issues so that he can keep us in bondage. He knows that as long as we are in bondage, we cannot be free to live healthy lives and fulfill the purpose that God has created for us. Acceptance is God's territory. Acceptance opens the door for God to come in and start the healing process.

In my own life, acceptance was not a place where I was beating the door down to come in. I was much more comfortable visiting denial. You see denial didn't mind me coming over there doing the same things over and over, going nowhere fast. I'd heard about the residence of acceptance, however, and over there real change was taking place. While I was in counseling, my counselor would suggest I try some grief counseling. This was really foreign to me because that was for people who were grieving and I didn't need that because my father had been dead for more than a decade. Yes, my father had been dead for more than a decade, and for more than a decade I'd been spinning my wheels over at denial's house. In my state of denial, I'd go from relationship or "situationship" to relationship/situationship seeking, seeking, seeking, but never finding. Let's park right here for a moment. Denial will make you think that going from relationship to relationship will cure your ailment when all it does is give you an opportunity to transfer baggage from place to place. The saying, "the best way to get over a man is to get under another" is misguided. The loss of anything, including relationships, involves a grieving process, and when we jump from relationship to relationship we do not allow ourselves to grieve, inevitably taking the baggage into future relationships.

Sometimes we think we are too busy to stop and take inventory of what is ailing us. Many of us stay in denial so long because we have other things that occupy our attention, making it easy to direct the necessary attention away from our own issues. These things can be careers, family, church, etc. You know the whole, "I don't have time to focus on my issues, I have three children who need raising" or "I don't have time to focus on my issues, I'm running the women's ministry at church." I say to think of it this way: how much better would you be at anything you do, if you do it as a whole, healthy person. Please understand, whether you know it or not, those deep-rooted issues that denial doesn't mind you running from are surfacing in some capacity, you're just too busy to really see the impact. In my own journey, I had to let go of the denial around not having an addiction. When my counselor suggested I join the Celebrate Recovery program, I was a bit apprehensive because I knew I had problems, but not with substance abuse, and I didn't want to make it seem I was being insensitive to those with "real" issues. Here is where I learned there are two types of addition: chemical and process. When a person has a chemical addiction they struggle with substances like alcohol or drugs. When a person has a process addiction, like me, they struggle with issues like emotional eating addiction, gambling, sex addiction, or porn addiction. In my case, the two I struggled with were an emotional eating addiction and sex addiction. Sex not so much from the enjoyment standpoint, but from the masking pain standpoint which is ultimately where most addiction whether chemical or process derive. Today, I proudly say, "Hello, my name is Samantha and I struggle with ..."

# CHAPTER 17

# ACCOUNTABILITY

Accountability is one of those areas that can make people feel very uncomfortable—mainly because it forces the person to take the finger they may point at another and turn it back on themselves. In my journey to freedom, accountability has forced me to realize I wasn't always the victim in my circumstances. There are certain situations in life where we have no control over bad things that happen to us and we truly are victims. Then there are situations where we do have control, but choose to not exercise it. In my own life, this has been so evident in my relationships. The saying, "people can only do what you allow," is not just a cliché; it's fact. I've had relationships where I allowed myself to be mistreated simply because my self-worth was pretty much non-existent, and I didn't think I could do better. However, that doesn't let me off the hook completely. The old adage says, fool me once, shame on you–fool me twice, shame on me. When I think about relationships, this phrase means if you hurt me once, that's on you and I didn't know you were going to do that. The second part of the phrase means oops you hurt me again, but this time it's my fault because I gave you another chance knowing what you were capable of. But what happens after that second chance, and the person who is supposed to love us hurts us again? Do we stay hoping and praying that change will come our way? I can tell you from my experience I've handed out far more chances than people have deserved.

When people hurt us once, we can hold the victim card, but if they hurt us multiple times continuing to do so, we are no longer victims, but enablers. In case you're not familiar with the definition of an enabler, an enabler is a person who encourages a behavior or helps something occur (that's negative or self-destructive). Perhaps that sounds harsh, but it's true. If someone mistreats you and you knowingly allow that to happen, when the chips fall down you have to step up and be accountable citing that yes they hurt me, but I didn't do anything to stop it. In my own life I've seen much hurt in the arena of "love," but when I really reflect on many of those situations, I realized that I stayed for far too long.

As I mentioned in the chapter, "Rebound," with that particular guy, I wanted to be angry with him for not treating me as I felt I deserved or as I wanted him to, but at the end of the day, the only person I could be upset with was me. In an exchange with him, I can remember having another breakdown where I just wanted him to "own" the hurt he caused me and was going on and on ranting about, "How would you feel if..." and "What would you do if...?" His response to me was not the answer I desired, but it was the answer that made the most sense. He simply said, "I would have left." There are no brownie points or merit badges being handed out for staying with a person who is not good for you or good to you. Now as a disclaimer, note that I'm not speaking about marriage here, that is another arena that I can't speak on (not right now at least. Look for the next book in a few years).

With the herpes condition, I've found that some people want to extend a level of sympathy to me, which is fine; however, since we're in the chapter on accountability, I must take responsibility for my part in contracting herpes. I was not raped. Even if in a broken state, I voluntarily slept with men without using protection. That is a risk one takes, and I had to pay the piper. That is accountability. As I close this chapter, allow me to leave you with a final thought. So many times in our lives we cry over situations that God never intended for us to be in from the beginning.

When I reflect on the situation with the guy who was incarcerated, I think about how many days and nights my tears almost choked me. There were so many nights I cried out to God asking why he had me in a situation that caused me so much pain. Then I would hear God say to me, "Samantha, why are you in that situation that causes you so much pain? You've been waiting for me to move when I've been waiting for you to listen." The Scriptures speak about being longsuffering or being able to patiently forbear, but that can become a slippery slope when we don't apply that principle in situations that God deemed appropriate. As I discussed earlier, I thought I was doing what God called me to do, but this ties back into the importance of being able to effectively discern the voice of God. I also bring this situation up in this chapter on accountability because sometimes we are the reason for our pain, and we have to own that. In the words of my father, "It's tight, but it's right." As Daughters of Freedom, we must first learn to be responsible for who we allow in our life, and what we allow to go on in our life.

# CHAPTER 18

# FORGIVENESS AND REPENTANCE

Forgiveness is one of those things that sounds so good in theory, but to actually put it into practice is challenging. From the Christian standpoint, forgiveness is something that God requires of us simply because He extends forgiveness to us continuously. What I've learned time and again is that forgiveness does not mean you excuse the person's behavior. It just means you choose to no longer allow the effects of unforgiveness to keep you hostage. Unforgiveness can keep you in a stagnant place of bitterness while the person who may have hurt you has moved on with their life. Let me put a pin here and tell you how hard it can be to forgive someone who has hurt you, yet has moved on with their life as though they did nothing to you. To be quite honest, the fleshly side of us wants the other person to hurt just as much as we do from their actions. Using my own life story, I was Facebook friends with the guy I'm certain I contracted herpes from. From his profile, it appeared all had been well with his life while I struggled to keep my sanity. For a very, very long time that just didn't seem fair to me. How could he get the "good life" while I struggled to keep mine together? Focusing on what is fair or not fair will keep you stagnant and in a place of bitterness. Remember, forgiveness is less about the other person, and more about setting you free from that stagnant place.

As I grow in my relationship with God, forgiveness becomes a bit easier whenever I need to extend it to someone else. Why? Because Scripture says, *"Vengeance is mine, sayeth the Lord. I will repay"* (Romans 12:19). Trust me when I tell you that God is not one who will lie. His word is true, and sometimes He will even allow you to see the vengeance bestowed on those who hurt you. I've witnessed this personally. Now this is just my personal assessment, but I don't believe God will allow you to witness the vengeance being bestowed on someone who hurt you, when you are still harboring a place of ill will towards them – you know, still having the "I want to see you hurt" attitude. Whenever I've had the opportunity to see vengeance it was after I'd come to a place of indifference about the situation. Indifference means you have moved past the situation and don't feel one way or another about the person or what they did to you. Because God is Holy and righteous He won't be a part of anything messy, and if He knows your heart still holds some bitterness, I don't believe He'd let you see the vengeance as your perception would be from a place without a pure heart.

One thing I definitely want to point out with forgiveness of others is the fact that you first have to acknowledge that you were hurt and that forgiveness is a process. Those two things have been big issues for me. Being a nice person, I always felt as though it was wrong for me to acknowledge my hurt and felt I needed to forgive people quickly. First, not acknowledging that somebody hurt you is denial, and you can't forgive what you can't admit happened.

Secondly, in my situations where I've tried to forgive quickly, usually in relationships, it hasn't been genuine. I'd often have this ulterior motive that if I "forgave" quickly, the person who hurt me would see how awesome I was and change their minds about me. That has never worked out and all it did was leave me more hurt, angrier, and more in a pit of unforgiveness. With the guy who ended the cycle of broken "situationships" in my life, because we technically weren't in a relationship, and he technically was always upfront about what he wanted and didn't want from me, I never felt justified in allowing myself to feel hurt over the situation. In our last, very nasty communication exchange with each other, he had no qualms about confirming my thought. It was in that moment that I realized I was justified in feeling hurt, whether he agreed or not. It was also in that moment that I realized we were done, and with that thought the tears began to flow. What is so ironic about that situation is the night the Holy Spirit told me he wasn't the one, I was crying into the pillow of my furniture, and the night I realized it was over, I was again crying into the pillow of my furniture, but this time the Holy Spirit whispered, "It's okay to grieve." I completely lost it at that moment as I realized that the One who had tried to warn me, loved me so much that even after I messed up, He would come back to comfort me. That is a true act of forgiveness.

> **I realized that the One who had tried to warn me, loved me so much that even after I messed up, He would come back to comfort me.**

For me, the subject of forgiveness of self has always been the most challenging of the two. I truly think I'm my worst critic and harder on myself than others. Going back to the root of my issues, when my father was alive I was a bit of a spoiled brat. After his death, I struggled with forgiving myself for not being a better, less demanding child. During the final days of his life, I can recall asking him to take me and my friends to get our nails done at a nail shop about an hour from where we lived. He told me he wasn't feeling well, but instead of being understanding I had a "teenage temper tantrum." I didn't know then that he was suffering from congestive heart failure and I would only have a short while longer with him. If I had known, I would have been less demanding, asking him what I could do for him instead of vice versa. After his death, I struggled with how my actions that day may have made him feel. It took me a very, very long time to forgive myself for not treasuring our time together.

It also took me a very long time to forgive myself for having unprotected sex and contracting herpes. Accountability has taught me that although I wasn't aware the person had herpes, it was still my decision to have unprotected sex. It was ultimately a decision I made that would change the course of my life, and for that, I had to learn to forgive myself. I had to learn to forgive myself for giving my body away countless times to men who didn't deserve to have shared that part of me.

When I moved to South Carolina my credit score was amazing, and in a matter of two years chasing after love would turn my financial world upside down. I had to learn how to forgive myself for making bad financial decisions to try and make a man love me who never had intentions on doing so. I had to learn to forgive myself for having such low self-esteem that I'd become an emotional manipulator lying to men about pregnancies so they would stay with me. I had to forgive myself for having such low self-esteem that I would even think of using something like miscarriages that are a real issue for a lot of women. We all have done things that today we go, "If I could do it all over again, I wouldn't." The fact of the matter is what's done is done. We can't dwell in the past, we can only move forward. Forgiveness will help us do just that.

Repentance and forgiveness are two words that you may hear used interchangeably, but in my opinion, they are very different especially when we talk about God. When I think about my journey to freedom, my mind goes back to the day I realized I needed to do more than ask for God's forgiveness; I needed to repent of my sins.

For years, I lived a life that was a direct contradiction to one that God expected of me. I remember one night in my War Room (we'll talk about that later), thinking about the mess I'd made in some of my life decisions and then wailing from a deep place asking for God's forgiveness. When we repent, it's not surface level. With repentance, we vow to God to make a diligent effort at turning away from the thoughts, actions, and behaviors that are not like Him. We know that our sins were nailed to the cross when Christ died, and because of that we are granted God's forgiveness and become recipients of His grace and mercy.

In my life, I've taken advantage of the fact that God would forgive me. What do I mean by that? I mean doing things in my life that I knew were not pleasing to God, but not feeling too badly about it because I'd just ask for His forgiveness afterward. Repentance says, "Lord, I'm done with that life, and not only am I asking for Your forgiveness, I'm vowing to turn away from those things that are not pleasing in Your sight." With repentance, we also acknowledge that we may need God's assistance in helping us stay clear of those traps we once used to fall into. God is a keeper of those who desire to be kept. We should remember that God loves us, and when we repent and ask for His forgiveness, He does just that. If we continue to have negative thoughts about things we have done, we need to remember that is condemnation from the enemy. God is one who convicts, showing you the error of your ways so you can correct them. The enemy is a condemner, one who continually beats you over the head and keeps you in a place of shame about your bad decisions. Kick the enemy in the shins, HARD, and tell him to go back to hell where he belongs.

CHAPTER 19

# BYE FELICIA, I MEAN SHAME

Merriam-Webster defines *shame* as "a feeling of guilt, regret, or sadness that you have because you know you have done something wrong."[4] Shame is what the enemy uses to give us amnesia as to what God has said about us. Shame and I have unfortunately become good friends over the past decade. It has been the enemy's number one tactic to keep me feeling like I had no value or self-worth, but the tide has turned. The enemy had me wound so tight, it was as though I thought people could look at me and tell I had herpes. I was always trying to hide behind the scenes, fearing that people could see the big scarlet letter on my chest. Shame is what kept me in dysfunctional relationships long after the expiration date because I thought to have anybody was better than nobody, and I needed to take what I could get. Shame had me seeking love on dating sites specifically for people with sexually transmitted diseases with the

---

4     Merriam-Webster. Accessed February 28, 2016. http://www.merriam-webster.com/dictionary/liability.

thought that the only way I'd date again was if I found someone who had herpes too—they really do have those sites. I'm not here to judge people who use those sites, I just feel our dating options shouldn't be put in a box simply because of a certain condition. One of my greatest reasons for writing this book was to kiss shame goodbye and turn the enemy's tactic against me back on him. Shame will attempt to strip you of your self-worth and the enemy was most definitely trying to do that to me and was succeeding in his efforts, honestly.

For years, I lived with the secret of having herpes. We live in a society where there is such negative stigma around sexually transmitted diseases, especially those that are incurable. This stigma is mainly due to people's lack of knowledge about the conditions. Society paints people with these conditions as nasty and dirty when the reality is that 1 in 3 people have herpes, so chances are some of those people who snub their noses may be carriers of the virus themselves, unknowingly. There were no physical signs that the guy I'm pretty sure gave it to me had the virus. I was very promiscuous during that time, but not so much that I'd voluntarily sleep with a man who had visible signs of a disease. I've heard people say things and have even read things on social media where people poke fun at others living with these conditions. In all honesty, I used to laugh at the people on those Valtrex commercials, until those people became me. An aside here is that we should always be careful what we choose to laugh at, we could very well be on the other side of that coin one day.

When I wrote this book, I felt it so important to have a visual to go with the message, so I had a photo shoot done. In the photo are two women, one kneeling bound in chains with her mouth taped shut, and the other free, reaching out to help the woman in bondage get up. For so long I lived as a woman chained to her past and silenced from speaking out against the lies of the enemy. One night as I prayed in a state of despair, God dropped in my spirit, "The enemy can't shame you with what you tell." From that moment forward, I made up in my mind that I'd do just that—I'd start telling my "secret."

> ## *God dropped in my spirit, "The enemy can't shame you with what you tell."*

I've been on a journey to freedom ever since. Every time I allowed the words to escape my mouth, I felt a link in the chain fall off. The enemy never desired for me to become a free woman, and just to further let him know what time it is, not only shall I dance in my freedom, but I'm on a quest to help other women "flip the script" so that they too can walk in freedom, living out the life that God purposed for them. The enemy can only shame us with things that are kept in the dark. I'm now a walker of the light, so see ya devil!

CHAPTER 20

# TAKING BACK YOUR SELF-WORTH

This chapter is a big part of my journey, so allow me to take my time. Shame can rob you of your self-worth and it did indeed do that for me, but after much self-discovery, I realized my self-worth took a hit before the herpes diagnosis. The first hit was with the seed the enemy planted back in 6th grade. Then he continued to water that seed, and when my father passed, that was just the icing on the cake. You see my father passed away from congestive heart failure. During the course of his illness, his doctors suggested that he consider receiving a heart transplant. My father had no desire to have another person's heart beating in his body so he opted not to have the transplant, knowing that death would likely be the outcome. This was hard for my mind to conceive. I was the apple of my father's eye. How could his desire to not want another person's heart inside of him override his desire to live longer and continue being the father that his baby girl needed? For a great deal of time, the enemy plagued my thoughts with, "If the man whose seed created me didn't think I'm worth living for, am I really worth anything?" In addition to trying to mask the pain of my father's death through men, I'd also use men to try and prove I was worth loving. As you can see from my story, that approach was not effective. For years, my abandonment issues left me feeling worthless and every time another man in my life would leave, it made me feel even more so. In my mind, I couldn't figure out if I was so valuable, why did none of the men in my life want to stay around?

After my herpes diagnosis, my self-worth plummeted. The diagnosis made me feel like I'd need to do even more to prove to men how worthy I was or how happy they should have been to have me in their lives. One of the most challenging things to do after learning about the herpes diagnosis was telling men I encountered. Granted, I could have kept it a secret, but it could have been a disaster had they contracted it as well, plus my integrity wouldn't allow me to keep it a secret even at the risk of rejection. Initially, none of the men I ever had to tell ran for the heels immediately, almost seeming okay with the condition, but they never stuck around or if they did, it was clear they didn't want anything serious with me.

I don't believe we can talk about self- worth without talking about self-esteem. When we lack self-esteem, we lack self-worth. The year that I started writing this book, my self-esteem had taken a few hits. I'd been more of a plus-size woman for most of my adult life and I'd, of course, meet men who preferred more slim women, but in my last relationship to my surprise, the guy had a preference for heavy women. After being together for a couple of months he finally told me he just wasn't attracted to me and couldn't get past the fact that I was too "slim." I was about a size 16 at this time. Perhaps I should've been flattered that he considered me "too slim," but instead I became a bit depressed not feeling good about myself at all. Here the enemy placed another "lie limb" on the tree of lies with thoughts like, "You'll never be good enough for anybody, whether fat or thin." For most of my life, I've been what society would consider plus size. To be completely transparent it saddens me how society treats those who are not "average" weight. Trying to lose and maintain weight is truly a battle that you cannot understand unless you've actually been overweight.

I think some look at a person who is overweight and thinks, "Well all they need to do is just stop eating so much and exercise, what's so hard about that?" Yes, that sounds simple, but what is forgotten in the equation is that many who are overweight have deeply rooted issues that connect to the weight, and until those issues are resolved, the simplistic healthy diet + exercise equation means nothing. How do I know? Because that was my story for a very long time. I knew how to lose weight, but what I didn't know how to do was address my triggers that caused me to become an emotional eater, hence causing me to be overweight. Whenever I was triggered emotionally I'd head to the nearest place to find some "comfort" food to soothe my hurt. I'm sure you're aware that "comfort" food rarely includes anything good for the arteries.

Life is full of challenges and using food as a coping aid for those challenges will surely tip the scale, but not in your favor. In my life, my lack of self-worth because of herpes has been a huge contributor to my weight struggle. I can recall asking one of my guy "friends" why it seemed that men were okay to sleep with me with the condition, but were never interested in commitment. His response to me is one I'll never forget. He said to me, "Men like to be reckless, and with herpes, they can't be reckless with you. If your body was 'right' you might have a better chance." In layman's terms, what he said was a man does not want to commit to someone they could potentially risk getting a disease from by having unprotected sex, but if I wasn't overweight that could increase my chances of helping them "forget" I had herpes. I can't even remember how many fast food drive-thrus I hit after that conversation with him.

Later in my adult life, I learned that my struggle with weight had a co-conspirator besides my emotional eating. I was diagnosed with Polycystic Ovarian Syndrome in 2007. One thing the condition does is makes it more challenging to lose weight. I've experienced the perfect storm in my life: an emotional food addiction + a health condition that adds to weight gain. Since we're speaking on the subject of worth, after being diagnosed with the Polycystic Ovarian Syndrome, my worth took another hit. Polycystic Ovarian Syndrome has many effects that can make a woman feel bad about herself. Two key things are the lack of a regular menstrual cycle and infertility issues. As a woman these are two things that we feel we are naturally designed to do, so not being able to can play with our self-worth.

In addition to those two things, one effect that has bothered me personally is the hair growth the condition causes. The moment I realized that I was buying razors not to shave my legs or arms, but the hair on my face, I thought I'd have a meltdown. I couldn't shake the thought that women are not supposed to grow hair on their face like men! I started to become so self-conscious about people getting close to my face, wondering if I'd shaved the whiskers low enough to not be noticeable. Whenever I would date a guy, I'd always shy away from his touching my face for fear of him feeling any stubble and thinking gross thoughts about me—I already felt gross with herpes alone. At this point, I was dealing Herpes, Polycystic Ovarian Syndrome, and being obese. Yes, the enemy truly thought he had served me a good cocktail. But he was and is a LIAR!

Society will make plus-size women feel that they have to settle for "whatever they can get," but again the devil is a liar! I totally love movies with romantic story lines and one of my favorites is, "Just Wright" starring Queen Latifah and Common. In the movie, Common plays this famous basketball player who falls in love with Queen Latifah's cousin, who in the movie is played by Paula Patton. Common falls for Paula because she is the slim one and by society's standards, likely the more "attractive" one. In the movie, he has an injury that threatens his career, and the one he chose first, Paula, drops him like a bad habit. Queen Latifah, who plays the role of a physical therapist, helps Common heal and get back to the game. During this process, he ends up falling in love with her. What I love about this story is that it is really representative of how plus-size women can be treated sometimes. Common was not interested in Queen Latifah at all until he got to know her, realizing she was the right one for him all along. I'm not saying a person shouldn't have a level of attraction to their mate, but what I am saying is that you can miss out on your good thing by focusing on the wrong thing.

Many times in my life, I've felt like a man's second option, but those days are over. I don't care what size I am, I will no longer settle for less than I deserve and less than I know the Father desires for me. When we become Daughters of Freedom, we understand that we deserve the cake and not just the leftover crumbs. Point. Blank. And the Period. I giggle inside when I think about the time I've spent trying to lose weight with the thought, "When I lose this weight, my ex will see what he lost."

> ***When we become Daughters of Freedom, we understand that we deserve the cake and not just the leftover crumbs.***

That is such wasted energy, and I'm a witness that going into it with that motive will often end in failure. When we learn to start walking in freedom, we realize that the choice to lose weight should be for our health and to take care of God's temple, not for the approval of man. When it comes to emotional eating, we must learn to find other avenues for dealing with our emotional triggers outside of food. If your weight is health-related, take steps to learn how you can be effective at getting to a healthy weight with your condition. At this point in my life, I take it one day at a time, recognizing that the weight didn't come on overnight, and it won't come off like that either. We have to be conscious and diligent daily at striving to be a better us, for us and the One who created us.

When I pause and look back over my life, I'm reminded of how much power I've given men to dictate my worth and how I felt about myself. I've had conversations with boyfriends who found it okay to inform me that their friends didn't know what he saw in me. I've run the gamut of guys who didn't like me because I wasn't slim enough to guys who didn't like me because I wasn't heavy enough. It does not matter whether they thought I was too big or too small. What mattered is what I thought of myself and more importantly, what God thought of me, and according to Him I was more than enough. I think we tread into dangerous territory when we give the authority to others to determine our worth.

As women, we place a great deal of emphasis on finding our worth in our relationships with men, especially marriage. I believe marriage is a beautiful entity, but somebody deciding to "put a ring on it" should not be one of the determining factors for your worth. When we receive the ring we should already be confident in the fact that the person chose to give us that ring because they know our worth is priceless too. I believe the movie, *War Room* illustrates this beautifully. I'll try not to spoil too much in case you haven't seen the movie, but in the storyline, the husband wasn't as nice as he could be to his wife. There came a point in the story where the husband just couldn't understand why his wife was being so nice to him, given how he had treated her. Her response to him was that she was God's before she was his and her contentment came from God, not him. To me, this said regardless of who we are independently my worth is not indicative of how you treat me, but of who God says I am. We should know who we are long before marriage.

If you lack self-worth, being a single woman or a woman in the dating world can be challenging. I read a Facebook post once that was very profound. It said, "You date on the level of your self-worth." I believe this is very true. Thinking back to my own situations I have endured far more than I should have in relationships because I did not value myself. When you have a high self-worth you will not have just anybody in your life treating you any type of way. Women with low self-worth say, "I'm just glad to have a warm body in my bed." Women with high self-worth say, "Before I choose anybody just to say I have somebody, I will be single and wait for the right person to come along." Thanks be to God I am finally in the latter of the two.

As I type these words I am almost 32. By society's standards, I should be married with a family by now. By my standards, I will wait on the Lord. It took me a long time to get to this place of worth, and it's still a work in progress. I will not jeopardize all that work by getting into a relationship with somebody who represents who I used to be just to say I'm not single. As an aside, there are worse things than being single, and that is getting tied up with someone who is not right for you. As another aside, the Bible speaks about being unequally yoked. As a woman heading into women's ministry, I understand the importance of waiting for a covenant with a man who is as passionate about Christ as I am. I also understand the importance of not getting tangled up in any more soul ties with men not for me. One liberating fact about being a single woman is that places you want to go will not turn you away because you don't have a date. If you want to go somewhere, go. Stop waiting for a man to come take you to those places. Life is too short for that. Besides, you never know what God wants to reveal to you on those self-dates. He can't do that while you sit at home and sulk about not having anyone to take you out. Take that outfit you've been saving out of the closet, make reservations for yourself, and go enjoy. Your confidence will thank you.

As God's Daughters of Freedom, we must be able to see ourselves the way that He sees us. When we see ourselves the way that God sees us, we realize that we are invaluable creatures who deserve nothing but the best. If you truly want to find an accurate assessment of your level of self-worth, ask yourself does what God says about me match up with what I say about myself. If the answer to that question is no, then there is time to do a self-worth adjustment. Spend time studying the Word of God and learning what He says about you.

If I may, allow me to drop in a quick history nugget that I think aligns with self-worth. Sara Baartman was a South African woman who was sold into slavery under the guise of coming to America for a better life, but when she arrived she was forced to take part in side-shows and human museums so people could come and stare at her voluptuous body. Sarah really didn't have a choice in her fate, but today as women we do, yet we voluntarily expose ourselves and our bodies to the world. I feel I'm a solid expert on self-worth, and I feel confident in saying exposing our bodies to the world does not line up with what God says about us. His word says our bodies are our temple and should be offered as a living sacrifice. Yes, we are all adults and can do, wear, and show what we want, but if we want to be respected, we must give something to respect.

Before I close this chapter out, I need to reaffirm a subject I talked about earlier in the book, and that is KEEP YOUR MONEY, HONEY! Women who lack self-worth are often co-dependent, meaning we often find ourselves in dysfunctional relationships where we deem it necessary to support or enable men. Women who lack self-worth thrive off of feeling needed and this includes being able to take care of men. I was quick to reach into my purse to help a man with his financial needs, even at the expense of my own. Allow me to give you a final example of why this is a horrible idea, at least unless you're married. After things ended with an ex, I tried to remain friends despite how we ended.

Let me put a pin here and do quick aside. There are no brownie points being handed out for trying to remain friends with exes. Sometimes all ties need to be severed and this includes the ones we try to hang on to with their families knowing it's just an excuse to hopefully stay relevant in the ex's eyes somehow. So back to what I was saying. With my ex, he felt he could still come and ask me for a loan, citing that he ran short on a bill. Because I was trying to "be friends" I agreed. I didn't have the money, but my family had just given me some birthday cash so I used that. Do you smell the stench of no self-worth dripping here yet? Something in my spirit was telling me not to do it, but I did it anyway. Immediately after the deposit was complete, I knew with conviction that I should not have agreed to give him the money—something wasn't right.

A few days later while perusing Instagram I oddly enough found a page I didn't know he had. I tell you, Instagram has truly exposed things in my life. When I went to his page, I found photos of him and another woman on what appeared to be a birthday outing for her. Not to be "Petty Labelle," but my birthday was that same week and when I mentioned that he forgot, he cited that he was going to get around to it, so I'm sure you know seeing those photos didn't sit well with me. Two things can be derived from this situation, either he used his bill money to take her out, hence needing a loan from me, or he used my money to take her out. Either way, it was a lose-lose situation for me. At that moment, I made up in my mind that no man outside of my husband would ever get a dime from me. A true man will find his own way.

Today, I thank God for bringing me to a place where I have found my self-worth. My new motto is I'm good enough because God created me in His likeness and image, point blank and the period. In lipstick on my mirror at home I wrote myself a little reminder that says, "I am more than enough," just in case I ever need a reminder. Perhaps you should try the mirror message. This can be an encouraging form of self-empowerment given most of us have to look in the mirror some point during our day. I used to feel like I had to work to earn people's love and that was directly attached to my worth. Then I came in contact with a person whose love I didn't have to earn. In fact, He loved me so unconditionally He gave His Son's life for mine.

As I walked my journey of freedom and started exposing the lies of the enemy, replacing them with what God said about me, everything about me started to change. Things I used to do, I wasn't doing anymore. In my past, I'd meet guys who desired to come over to my house way past a respectable hour, but I'd agree simply because I was just happy they were interested in coming over at all. Today, my high self-worth self will tell you if a guy gets invited over at all, he will be coming at a respectable hour. If he has opposition to that, it's his problem, not mine. I can remember having a conversation with the last guy in my life and his telling me how he was really starting to see the true me. He wasn't saying that in a positive manner, but it was actually true. Every encounter he'd had with me was with a woman who was infected with the enemy's lies, and because of that had NO self-worth. At the end of our journey, God started doing a new thing, and the guy was finally seeing me. He was seeing the me that God always desired me to be, the me that stood on the Scriptural text, "Greater is he that is in me than he that is in the world" (See 1 John 4:4), the me that finally understood that I didn't need an earthly man to validate me, or make me feel worthy to be loved.

One of my favorite gospel songs is by Anthony Brown called, "Worth." The song perfectly describes how much God deems us worthy to be loved. With the herpes condition, another "lie limb" the enemy put on the tree he planted in my life was constant worrying about if I'd ever be somebody's something special. Then I learned to embrace the significance that I was already and would always be somebody's something special, so much so that He gave His life for mine. As a Daughter of Freedom, I am now completely confident that before I let another imposter into my life, I will stay single being content and completely tucked into the one who was sent, my Savior, Jesus Christ. When it's my time, He will send me the one who found me by diligently seeking after Him.

**Then I learned to embrace the significance that I was already and would always be somebody's something special, so much so that He gave His life for mine.**

Let me close this chapter with a funny story. Recently, my doctor gave me a refill for Valtrex, which is the prescription for herpes. The day I went to the pharmacist, I picked up the Valtrex and a cortisone cream for my arm. When the pharmacist began telling me about the cortisone, she spoke in a normal voice, but when she got to the Valtrex I noticed that her tone dropped so low I could barely hear her. In my mind, I thought, "Ma'am I know my worth and I am no longer ashamed." A few different times I've heard pastors and speakers use the analogy of a $100 dollar bill and its worth. It didn't matter if the $100 bill was crumpled, stepped on, or even torn apart, at the end of the day, it was still spendable and its value the same. This is the same for you, beloved. It doesn't matter what you've been through, your value has never changed. Ladies, Daughters of Freedom know their worth, and if after reading this chapter, you still have some uncertainty, allow me to help you out – YOU ARE GOOD ENOUGH! In fact, you are MORE than good enough! Why? Because God said so, and as stated in His word in Genesis, everything He created was good!

# CHAPTER 21

# GROWING YOUR RELATIONSHIP WITH GOD

In order to gain true freedom, you must have a solid relationship with God—there is really no way around it. Anything else will only provide temporary freedom, and we don't want that. I've had an awareness of God for as long as I can remember due to growing up in the church. However, I've learned that there is a difference between knowing *about* God and actually knowing God. I believe when we know about God, He is someone we hear about in church but seems to be abstract. When we know God, it's not totally based off of what we've heard in church, rather what we've gleaned from an intimate, personal relationship with Him. When I became an adult, I realized that life is full of challenges, and it was those challenges that made me realize I could not do life alone. It was during the most difficult times of my life that I found out acting in my own strength was not sufficient and I needed to call on this person I'd heard so much about growing up. What I realized is that God was always there with open arms waiting for me, but He is a gentleman and will never force Himself on us. That is why we have free will. It is up to us to decide whether we want to come to know the Lord or not. My story is that for so long I had an emptiness inside of me that I was trying to fill in all the wrong places. One thing we should be cognizant of is that the only person who can fill voids effectively in our lives is God. Trying to get others to do so is an unfair burden. When we have God as a solid foundation, then we can effectively build other healthy relationships.

> **One thing we should be cognizant of is that the only person who can fill voids effectively in our lives is God. Trying to get others to do so is an unfair burden.**

One of the things I think we fail to realize is that growing a relationship with Christ is just like the growth of any relationship. Some find it hard to equate the two when in a human relationship there are two physical bodies, but in a relationship with God, there is you the human being, and God the spiritual being. Think about this from the standpoint of getting into a relationship with a new guy. The relationship would not thrive if the two of you didn't communicate and spend time together. Nor would it thrive if one of you was always the giver and the other always the receiver. This is the same with God. Many times we say we want to know God and hear His voice, but how can we know someone or their voice if we don't spend time with them. Furthermore, we want God to speak to us and let us in on some of His "secrets," but why would He do that with someone He doesn't know.

This is a good place to also point out that when you establish a relationship with God, it's a process. We all came into this world as infants and had to eat baby food, and we only started eating table food as we got older. It's the same with our relationships with Christ. It is not expected that immediately you will be able to quote every Scripture in the Bible or know definitively that you're always hearing God's voice. There are baby Christians and there are adult Christians. It doesn't matter where you fall in the journey; the importance is that you are always moving forward in your journey.

Growing up I can remember both my mother and father having no issue running and shouting all over the church as though something had caught their feet on fire. To be honest, back then I was a little embarrassed, but today I have a better understanding of what caused their feet to seem to be on fire. It was the One Scripture describes as the "Comforter"—the One who came to be with us after Christ ascended back to Heaven. He is the same One who lives on the inside of us acting as our compass in this life. He is the One who is so sweet. When His presence falls in the room, words cannot find the proper definition to describe the experience. Yes, He is truly the "Comforter" or better known as the Holy Spirit.

In the early stages of my walk with Christ, I'd find myself to be a quiet worshipper, not really wanting to draw attention to myself. But as I got older and my relationship matured, I began to care less about who saw me with my hands raised and a tear stained face—I knew who had been good to me, and I was no longer afraid to worship Him with my whole heart! The Word of God says to make a joyful noise unto the Lord! I believe it's when you get to that phase, that you truly allow yourself to be vulnerable enough for the Holy Spirit to come and see about you. What do I mean by that? Well, I used to watch a lot of Benny Hinn services on television and I'd always be in awe of how it seemed that everyone there was touched by the Holy Spirit. Some would speculate that it was just for television, but I'm a believer that the Holy Spirit will come and indwell in places where the people's hearts are receptive. In fact, God says so in His word,

"For where two or three are gathered together in my name, there am I in the midst of them" (Matthew 18:20). I have been blessed to have my own experiences like that.

Every year I attend a women's retreat in the mountains of Tennessee, and every year I'm always amazed at how the Holy Spirit dwells among us. I believe the reason for this is because we all come with an expectancy to bask in His presence. The first time I had an unexplainable experience with the Holy Spirit, I remember telling my friend it was as though my worship bubbled out of me like uncontrollable lava. The more the words, "Hallelujah, Jesus" rolled off my lips, the more excited my spirit man became. It was like something truly being poured out of me at the Master's feet. It was in those moments, that I now am aware that in my worshipful outpouring, God was pouring more of Himself and more of His anointing into me. What a blessing! Every encounter I have with the Holy Spirit makes me feel as though God is transforming something in me. I'd always feel closer to Him than I did before. When reading and meditating on His word, He would open up the Scripture like never before.

There is much controversy today about God and the Bible, but what I know with conviction is that being able to know what it feels like to bask in the presence of God will change your perception on anything you thought you knew. You can't have a real experience with the Holy Spirit and question whether God is real. You just can't! Normally, when we fall in love, we have a tendency to become a bit selfish, not wanting to share the individual with someone else. In this case, I have a great longing for all, especially God's daughters to experience this relationship. I don't want to keep this goodness to myself. Perhaps you have a desire to a start a relationship with the sovereign One or need to rededicate your life. If so, before we go any further, let's pray right now— yes, right smack dab in the middle of the book.

### *<u>Prayer of Salvation</u>*

*Dear Heavenly Father, I am confessing to You that I am a sinner and believe that the Lord Jesus Christ died for my sins on the cross and was raised for my justification. I do now receive and confess Him as my personal Savior. In Jesus' name, Amen.*

Maybe after reading or reciting the prayer you're wondering, "Is that it?" Yes, that's it. Perhaps the prayer seems simple, but everything doesn't have to be complex for it to be impactful—God heard you.

If I may, I'd like to share a few areas with you that have been so important for me on my Christian journey. The first is getting in the Word of God. The Word of God is the firm foundation for a relationship with God. You can't have a genuine relationship with God if you don't spend time reading, studying, and meditating on His word. The King James Version is likely the most common version, but because of the way it is written it may be a little more difficult to understand for those who are new to the Bible. However, today there are a variety of translations that make it easier for the believer to understand the Word of God. Let me tell you that regardless of the translation, the Word of God is the same yesterday, today, and forevermore. God has given many promises to His children, but if you don't spend any time in the Word of God you will have no knowledge of those promises. The enemy trembles at the Word of God, so it is good to have it tucked in your heart for when the enemy comes with his mess. When we are in prayer, God likes for us to give Him back His word; we cannot do this if we don't know it. As our relationship grows with God so will our understanding of His word.

It is not expected that when you become a believer, you will be able to quote every Scripture that day. If I can go deeper, it's not just about being able to quote the Scripture, it's about being able to have an understanding of Scripture and how to apply it to your life. I can remember early in my walk with Christ I thought I was doing something by just picking up the Bible, reading a chapter or two, then getting up and going on about my business, checking it off of my "to-do list" for the day. During that time, I was under the impression that reading the Bible was something I needed to do so God could be proud of me, but I wasn't really gleaning anything from what I read. Today, I understand that reading the Word of God is not something to do out of obligation; it is something to do so my soul can be fed the sustenance it needs for this life. When I grasped this fact, I realized instead of zooming through a chapter or two, I needed to spend time chewing on just a few Scriptures at a time. When we rush through reading God's Word, we can miss what He is trying to tell us through His Word. I implore you to take your time with the Word of God. Let me tell you that now I read the Word of God not out of obligation but out of desire.

The second area I would like to address is getting connected with other believers. Unfortunately, the world we're living in now doesn't seem to show a genuine reverence for God or Christianity, and because of that, it is important that you are in fellowship with others who believe like you do so that you are not tempted to fall back into old ways based on your external surroundings. When we become followers of Jesus Christ, we are in the world but not of the world. This means that although we have to exist in this world we don't have to allow the things of this world to poison us. This may be a hard pill to swallow, but you can't become a follower of Christ and continue to fellowship with those whose behaviors are in direct contradiction to the Word of God. I believe there is an exception for this if you are in outreach ministry and God is calling you to try and win souls that way. I'm also not telling you to end all your friendships with those who are not saved, as you can be a light for them and possibly lead them to Christ. What I am saying is that you can be that light and not do the old things you used to do. When you become a follower of Jesus Christ, you are choosing a side. That means there can be no straddling the fence. You can't have one foot in the world and one foot in the church.

I've heard much controversy about people leaving the church because of the perception that there are more hypocrites in the church than in the world. I cannot say whether this is true or not, but what I can say is that even if you're not going to a physical dwelling every Sunday morning, you should be finding some way to connect with other believers. In addition to reading God's Word on your own, you need to be hearing it from other platforms. This feeds your spirit and grows your faith. Scripture says in *Romans 10:17*, *"So then faith cometh by hearing, and hearing by the Word of God."* I believe this Scripture references what God speaks to you personally, but also what you glean from being fed the Word of God through a Bible-based platform.

When you choose a ministry to connect with, you want to ensure it's one where the Word of God is coming forth from the pulpit. I should also note that as you mature in your Christian walk, you may not stay at the same ministry. In my own journey, I know as an infant in Christ I needed to be connected to a church where the Word was broken down so I could understand it with ease. Today, as I've matured in my walk, I'm interested in a Word that doesn't bring just a surface level message but digs a little deeper. If I had to give a solid word of advice, it would be to connect with a ministry that is truly preaching the Word of God from the Word of God. This is why it is so important that you are rooted in Scripture. You need to be able to know if what you're hearing is actually the Word of God. When it comes to getting connected, the best thing to do is to pray and ask God what you should do, and let Him lead you to where He wants you to be. I can assure you that trying to live a Christian life in isolation is the easiest way for you to falter.

The third thing that has been beneficial in my walk with Christ is fasting. I believe spiritual fasting is so important to help sustain us in our walk with Christ. During a spiritual fast, we have the opportunity to sacrifice something in exchange for getting closer to God. In a world that is ever-hustling and bustling, it can sometimes become challenging to hear from God; that's when we need to hit the "pause" button and go into a time of fasting and praying. Even Jesus, when He was in the wilderness fasted for 40 days and 40 nights. Jesus' fast consisted of going without food. This is often the way many believers fast as well, but I believe during a fast it doesn't necessarily just have to be food. We can sacrifice something that we find is a major distraction in our lives or something we think it would be hard to go without.

During the time that I wrote this book, I went on a 45 day fast from social media. I appreciate the usefulness of social media, but at times I can find myself too absorbed. The purpose of the fast was for me to confirm what I heard God telling me regarding what He wanted me to do. Not only did He give me confirmation, but He also set me free from the lies of the enemy which would be so important for the journey that He has for me. In a season of fasting and praying, the benefit will far outweigh whatever you sacrificed.

The fourth thing that has also been valuable in my walk with Christ is understanding the importance of sowing. I saved this one for last because it can make folks a little uncomfortable, which is a good thing. Tithing is one of those areas that the Bible gives specific instructions on, yet there is much controversy in the church on whether what God said still stands since the Scripture that specifically speaks about tithing is in the Old Testament. Some don't feel it is necessary to live by the rules in the Old Testament because of Jesus' sacrifice in the New Testament. However in *Matthew 5:17, Jesus said, "Don't misunderstand why I have come. I did not come to abolish the law of Moses or the writings of the prophets. No, I came to accomplish their purpose"* (NLT). I interpret this to mean that we should be cognizant of all of the Word of God and not just choose either the Old Testament or the New Testament. *Malachi 3:10 says, "'Bring the whole tithe into the storehouse, that there may be food in my house. Test me in this,' says the Lord Almighty, 'and see if I will not throw open the floodgates of heaven and pour out so much blessing that there will not be room enough to store it'"* (NIV). During this time a tithe was to be 10%. What I interpret this Scripture to mean is that we are to sow our first fruits or the first of any increase we receive back into the Kingdom of God.

I'd also like to add that when I talk about first fruits, this doesn't always reference money. Our first fruits can be spending time with God when our feet hit the floor in the morning. I can remember a time where I'd try to spend all my time with God in the evenings, and sometimes I'd be so tired from the day I knew I was giving God my leftovers. What would my life look like if He did that to me? In Malachi 3:10, God is saying when we give Him our first fruits, we should watch how He will pour blessings into our lives. I am a living witness of this Scripture being true and have seen the impact of both sides. When I was tithing or sowing into the Kingdom of God, I could see His blessings left and right, and I'm not just talking monetarily.

We must be mindful that God's blessings run much deeper than just money. I'm also referring to opportunities, healings, and peace. I've also been on the side of not tithing, allowing the enemy to make me think I couldn't afford to tithe because I just had too many bills. Let me tell you what I learned here: even when I didn't tithe, I still didn't have enough to pay my bills. I can remember the hardest financial year of my life where it seemed I was on the brink of losing everything, and my mother and I had a conversation where she asked me if I was still tithing. I shamefully told her no, and she confidently told me that is where I went wrong. That day I made up in my mind that I would never stop tithing regardless of what my situation looked like. I haven't and God has continued to keep His end of the bargain. What I feel is the difference between the Old and New Testament concerning tithing is that in the Old Testament, tithing was a requirement and something people did out of obligation, but in the New Testament, tithing should be an act of gratitude and thanksgiving for what God has done. We need to remember that He is the source and the One who gave us the resource of which He only asks for 10% back. Not because He needs it, but because He wants to know if we trust Him in every area of our life.

Allow me to also say this: if you give to God out of obligation and do it with a begrudging heart, you may as well keep it. As I just said, God does not need our money, and He knows whether we are giving from a cheerful or resentful place. In the Word of God, He requires a 10% tithe. Today, some have questioned whether the need to give 10% is still necessary or if God simply requires whatever is placed on your heart to give. Whatever amount you give is between you and God, but please understand that there can be no harvest reaped where no seeds have been sown. Some may say that their life is blessed even though they don't tithe. I believe that is because God is full of grace and mercy, but think about how much more blessed your life could be if you acted in obedience to the Word of God.

I accepted Christ into my life at an early age but rededicated my life to Him as an adult, and in fact, I rededicate my life to Him daily. Falling in love with Jesus is truly the best thing I have ever done. I'll touch on this a bit later in the book, but one thing you should know is that when you accept Christ as your Savior, you have turned your back on the enemy and he will not be pleased with that to the point where his quest will become how to derail you from your newfound life with Christ. But what I love about God is that no matter how hard the enemy tries, when we become born again, nothing, not even the enemy's tactics can separate us from His love. I encourage you to ask God to lead you to a holy vessel where you can truly be fed the Word of God and get in fellowship with other believers. I know there is a lot of talk about the church not being what it's supposed to be, but don't let that deter your quest.

> *No matter how hard the enemy tries, when we become born again, nothing, not even the enemy's tactics can separate us from His love.*

In a world where the enemy is running to and fro seeking whomever he can devour, you need to have a solid foundation in Christ, but also a place you can go where people are on the same journey as you, encouraging you every step of the way.

Deciding to follow Christ does not mean you will have a life free of challenges (go back to what I said at the beginning of this paragraph), but what it means is that you will have the best person walking with you hand in hand through those challenges. There will be times where you may feel like walking in the light is the road less traveled or even the less popular road, but remember what the ultimate benefit is—eternal life. I will even go as far to say that you won't even have to wait until Heaven to see some of the jewels that God desires to drop into your life. I believe He desires to give us some pieces of Heaven right here on earth. As my pastor from my hometown often says, "Serving the Lord will pay off after a while."

Once you become a child of God, what do you do may be your next question. Jesus said in *Matthew 9:37, "The harvest truly is plenteous, but the labourers are few."* Now that you've come into relationship with God, what will you do to give back to the Kingdom? You can't receive such a gift and not strive to help others find that gift. My writing this book and doing ministry work is not for my own benefit, it is for the uplifting of the Kingdom of God, and to share with my brothers and sisters this joy I've found in the hopes that they will find it for themselves as well.

## CHAPTER 22

# FINDING YOUR PURPOSE

Suicide. Okay, I know you're probably thinking how does she have a chapter about finding your purpose that begins with talking about suicide. Well, before I discovered what God created me for, I had rock bottom moments where thoughts of suicide consumed me. Suicide is one of those words that most people will never acknowledge has crossed their mind—perhaps not the actual act of wanting to kill oneself, but simply not being able to find the will to live. When I started writing this book I was going through one of the hardest years of my life. Very few people knew that I was struggling to get out of bed most days, and when I did I was literally having to focus on putting one foot in front of the other. I was the woman of God who always had inspirational and encouraging posts on Facebook, the one whose posts were shared by others stating how much they were encouraged, yet I wasn't able to apply those things to my own life in that season. I'd come across heart-wrenching stories of other people's struggles that would make me snap out of my "pity party," but it would only be temporary. I'd go to the gym to try and work off how I felt, but immediately after I'd go through any fast food drive thru and get the item with the most calories. Who cared if I had a heart attack? That would not have been suicide and I wouldn't be sent to hell since that's what religion taught me. The storms in my life had truly worn me out and I felt like I was losing my fight. If this was "living" I was ready to go home to be with my heavenly Father. Then one day something happened. The Holy Spirit gave me an eye-opening revelation! Regardless of what my circumstances appeared to be, if God didn't have a purpose for my life why would He have saved me from a hole in my heart that should have killed me. As a matter of fact, let me share that story with you now.

In 2011, I was sitting in the Hartsfield-Jackson Atlanta International Airport preparing to fly back home from a business trip. As I waiting for my plane to board, I started experiencing a rapid heart rate that I'd never felt before. It unnerved me so much I wasn't sure whether to board the plan or go the ER. I ended up boarding the plane, but once back in North Carolina, I made a visit to my primary care doctor who suggested I may have just been experiencing anxiety. I wasn't okay with that diagnosis and requested she send me for further testing. She sent me for a chest X-ray, and on the X-ray they found that the right side of my heart was significantly enlarged. This prompted my primary care physician to send me to the cardiologist.

At the cardiologist, I was made aware that they would need to pump a substance through my vein to see how my heart was functioning. Prior to this procedure, the nurse conducted an echocardiogram which is essentially an ultrasound of the heart. I can recall her stepping out of the room to get the equipment for the test, but when she stepped back in she said to me, "Before we do this test, I want the doctor to take a look." When he came into the room and looked at my ultrasound pictures, he said to me, "You have a hole in your heart. It's a good thing we didn't do the vein test. That substance would've created a bubble surely causing you to have an aneurysm." Look at God!

My diagnosed condition was an atrial septal defect which is a congenital birth defect. I was born with this condition and it needed to be fixed as soon as possible or I would surely end up in heart failure within the next two years. Now let me place a pin here. Four years prior to this event, I can recall during an annual check-up, my doctor telling me she heard a heart murmur. I got an echocardiogram then as well, but was told the murmur was harmless—well, it, in fact, was not. For four years that hole in my heart was growing, but God sustained me. I ended up needing to have heart surgery to close the hole in my heart. I never, ever thought I would be told by a physician that I needed heart surgery.

The procedure was supposed to be an outpatient procedure; however, the hole in my heart was so large I had to spend a night in the hospital for monitoring. I did not need to have open heart surgery to have the hole closed; instead, the procedure involved running a catheter from my groin to my heart. This was definitely a less invasive procedure but equally dangerous as the catheter was inserted through a major artery in my groin which could potentially cause me to bleed to death after surgery if I wasn't extremely careful. Today I live with a patch inside my heart that closed the hole. The swelling no longer exists and my heart is perfectly healthy.

I shared this story to emphasize that when God has a purpose for our life, death can try but it will fail. To this day, the doctors are trying to figure out how I lived 27 years with a hole the size of the one I had in my heart. Whenever life tries to make me feel depleted, I remind myself that God did not save my life only for me to be defeated. Regardless of what you've been through, if you are reading this book, it means you are a survivor and that God has spared your life for a reason. You are not a victim. You are victorious! Beloved, God is the giver and taker of life. If He sees fit to continue waking you each morning that means He still has a work for you to do and it's not time for death to claim your earthly body. Thoughts of not wanting to live come from the enemy!

---

***If you are reading this book, it means you are a survivor and that God has spared your life for a reason. You are not a victim. You are victorious!***

---

Remember, the Word of God says that the enemy comes only to steal, kill and to destroy. He knows that God has a GREAT plan for our lives and he will do everything in his power to keep that from happening. God's Daughters of Freedom understand that life will have its challenges and that we must be intentional when it comes to getting rid of the enemy. We can only do that by building a solid relationship with Christ which includes spending time in prayer, meditation, fasting, and studying His Word.

I wish I could tell you that you will be proficient at these things overnight, but you won't. Remember what I said in the previous chapter, it takes baby steps. However, be diligent and watch how God moves in your life. While we are on the subject of the hole I had in my heart, allow me to make a quick aside. One day as I sat thinking about the hole in my heart I said to God, "God, You created me, why would You purposefully leave a hole in my heart?" He then placed in my spirit that He made the hole so that He could come back and fix it 27 years later. If it was fixed at birth, medical science could've called it "routine," but 27 years later they could only call it "God." Some situations in life can cause us to have a "why me" attitude when perhaps we should be humbled that God saw fit to use us for His glory.

One of my favorite Scriptures is *Philippians 1:6 which states, "Being confident of this very thing, that he which hath begun a good work in you will perform it until the day of Jesus Christ."* I love this Scripture as it aligns with purpose because it identifies that God has indeed put a work in you, which means you have an assignment. I spent so much of my life trying to find out what it was that God created me to do, and I know I'm not alone in that situation. Once I graduated from college, my biggest goal was to get a good 9-5 gig. Well, God blessed me with that 9-5, but there was still something in me saying there was more to life than this. I started to resent the office job I'd so longed for. One day while at work, I had a woman come into my office and say, "You're too bright to be in this office. People can't see you in here." It was so ironic because that is truly how I had been feeling—like a caged bird who desired to be free. I believe many of us have been taught that getting a good education and having a good career is the key to life. For some, that may be the case, but for others, we've been created for something else. We just have to find what that something else is. This is where we have to take the time to get in touch with the One who created us. I sometimes wonder if I'd taken the time or even been knowledgeable enough to know I needed to seek God's face on the direction of my life would I be sitting with $167,000 in student loan debt for degrees that didn't necessarily line up with my purpose. I thank God that I now know what my calling is. I, of course, don't know how all the details work out, but that I don't need to know. I walk by faith and not by sight.

This may seem too simple, but often times our purpose is tied to our passion. What is it that moves you and you would do even if money was not involved? For many people, this usually turns into a hobby because again we've been taught that the only way to gain success is in corporate America. Many times people are afraid to move into their passion because they wonder if they will be able to sustain financially, but I heard a pastor say that profit will follow purpose. Another one of my favorite Scriptures says, your gift makes room for you and will bring you before great men (see Proverbs 18:16). As I interpret this Scripture, I understand it to mean that what God has gifted you with will bring you before powerful people, and I'm certain there are some coins attached to that. I'd like to share something that I feel is helpful when we've found what our purposes are.

When we are not completely sure what our purpose is we have the tendency to be involved in so many things, many times literally running ourselves into the ground and spreading ourselves too thin. I've often heard people describe me as dependable and able to be relied on. Because of that, I've found myself getting involved with many activities that did not line up with my purpose simply because I had a "good heart." When you identify what God is calling you to do, there are going to be times when you will have to simply exercise the word "no." Sometimes being busy can be a tactic of the enemy to keep you from fully focusing on what God has assigned you to do. My advice here is to always seek His counsel from the smallest detail to the largest.

When I was writing this book, I knew with conviction that this was one of my assignments from God, yet many times it seemed as though I was trying to fight for time to write due to many other commitments I had. When God has put you on assignment, the enemy has no desire to see that assignment come to fruition and will put everything he can in your way. Look at your situation closely moving forward and ask yourself, is this part of my purpose or a distraction? Please be mindful that every opportunity, even one that looks good, may not be for you. I don't want to give the illusion that we shouldn't support each other especially as sisters because I believe we absolutely should, but it has to be done in a fashion where we can be supportive but not neglecting our own calling. One thing about me, I will help whoever, whenever, and many times it was because I was just a helpful person, but sometimes it was because I wanted to please the other person.

When I started writing this book I had to become real clear on whose approval I was ultimately seeking, and the answer was the One who gave me the assignment—God. Whenever God has placed something inside of you, I like to think of it as it relates to the birthing process. God will place "babies" inside of us, and when it comes time for labor, we have to ensure our focus is on pushing that baby out. When a woman is in actual labor, the last thing she is thinking about is going over to the next room to help the other mother push her baby out. That doesn't mean she doesn't care about the other mother having a successful delivery, it just means she has to focus on her own delivery.

Since we are on the analogy of the birthng process, let me discuss that a bit further. When a woman first finds out she is pregnant she is normally ecstatic. This is how it can be when we have the "aha" moment about our purpose, realizing that God has planted a seed in us. At the onset of pregnancy, a woman's hormone levels go crazy and can cause morning sickness. After you've found your purpose, it may not directly match up with what you do on a day-to-day basis, so perhaps you begin struggling to try to figure out how you're going to go from corporate America to full-time author and motivational speaker. Those conflicting thoughts can become overwhelming causing you "morning sickness."

In the second trimester, many women have moved past the sickness phase into the phase of actually being able to feel their baby move. This can bring true joy with the thought that a living being is on the inside of them. When you've come into the second trimester of your "purpose pregnancy," you'll likely be in a phase where the morning sickness has subsided, because you've turned your cares over to God, and now you're starting to feel the baby move thanks to the nuggets and direction God has been dropping into your spirit.

In the third trimester, the woman can start to become uncomfortable. She can be plagued by sleepless nights because the baby is getting so big, and weird things are beginning to happen to her body as it prepares for delivery. This is the same for your "purpose pregnancy." In your third trimester, the baby God has been growing gets so big you can barely sleep with the anticipation of its arrival. When it is time for actual labor, some women experience long hours to the point of fatigue and they feel they just can't go on, but they have people around them encouraging them to push until the baby makes their debut. This is the same for your "purpose pregnancy." When it's time for labor and delivery, the process may feel so grueling that you don't think you can make it, but you should be surrounded by people who can keep you encouraged until God's baby is born through you.

As an aside, in my own process of my "purpose pregnancy," I think of my publisher as my midwife, the one who will help take my manuscript and turn it into an actual book. I think of my family and friends as those supporters who keep me encouraged when the enemy tries to grow another "lie limb" around nobody caring about my story. After a baby is born, they change the lives of all they come in contact with. This is the same for your "purpose pregnancy." God placed it inside of you to change the lives of all who come in contact with you. It is for His glory and your good.

When we identify our purposes, let us not forget that there will be some work required. When a woman becomes pregnant she can't just do nothing and expect to have a healthy baby. She has to do her part by going to doctor's appointments, taking her vitamins, exercising, etc. This is the same for "purpose pregnancies." Many times we have our "aha" moments and become so excited praying, "Lord, please do it" and "I'm waiting on you, Lord," when often times I believe God is saying, "What are you doing?" and "I'm waiting on you." In James 2, Scripture tells us that faith without work is dead. This simply means that while we're asking God to do His part, we also need to be prepared to do our part. Sometimes doing our part may require us stepping out of our comfort zone.

When I left North Carolina to move to a state where I had no family or friends that was definitely stepping out of my comfort zone. I'm here to tell you with conviction that it was the best decision I ever made in my life. Yes, there were a lot of challenging, uncomfortable moments, but it was in those moments that God was growing me. Staying in a place of comfort can stunt your growth and that is not what God desires. It's because I was bold enough to step outside of my comfort zone that God was able to do a complete renovation in my life. As Daughters of Freedom, we must understand that God wants to take us higher, but He can only do that when we make up in our minds to choose faith over fear. God is not one who can lie and He said in His Word, *"'For I know the plans I have for you,' declares the Lord, 'plans to prosper you and not to harm you, plans to give you hope and a future'"* (Jeremiah 29:11).

Before I close this chapter out, I need to say that when we've identified our purpose, we need to understand that there will be a pruning process. Pruning is essentially a gardening skill, but also beneficial when discussing life. When pruned correctly, the plant will experience healthy growth. If a plant is not pruned, its growth can be stunted. Pruning involves cutting, which can be painful, but is necessary for God to get us ready for where He is taking us. Take it from me, don't fight Him just go with the flow. During the pruning process, we also need to understand that there may be a parting of the ways between ourselves and people currently attached to us. This is not personal, but some people simply cannot go where God is trying to take you. Once again, take it from me, don't fight Him on this. Allow me to leave you with one final thought in regards to finding your purpose. This life we have is not the dress rehearsal; this the show. There are so many reality shows on T.V. and I myself have been guilty of watching one or two, but do we want to spend our lives watching others live theirs, or do we want to aspire to find out what God wants us to do with ours? I heard something profound once regarding how much untapped potential is in the graveyard— how many die not even having tapped into what God called us to do. For me, my focus is on striving to leave everything God has poured into me on this earth. As Daughters of Freedom, I know God has poured something into you as well, and prayerfully you will join me on the quest to find out what that is.

# CHAPTER 23

# DISCERNING THE VOICE OF GOD

*"My sheep hear my voice, and I know them, and they follow me."*
John 10:27 (NIV)

As a Christian, one area where I struggled greatly was around discerning God's voice. During the course of my writing this book I was participating in a Bible study on discerning the voice of God. What I began understanding from the Bible study was that the Holy Spirit had been speaking to me for many years, but I was hitting the override button not being certain if it was the voice of God that I was hearing. Struggling with self-worth issues, I honestly didn't even believe I was worthy enough for God to speak to me. Allow me to point out how much that thought is from the enemy. When we accept Christ as our Savior we receive His Holy Spirit who indwells in us and guides us in this life. When I sit and reflect, there have been a few different cases where the Holy Spirit has spoken to me as it pertains to my relationships with men. You've heard me reference throughout the book the scenario with myself and the guy I specifically heard God say wasn't the one. I did not take heed. Many times we think we're not hearing the voice of God because it may be different than what we really want to hear. I didn't want to hear that guy wasn't the one, I wanted him to be—he was all I had in an unfamiliar state. When I heard the Holy Spirit tell me the guy wasn't the one, that was my cue to sever ties, but instead, I continued my pursuit of him and less than a year later I'd find myself in the worst financial distress of my life.

> **Many times we think we're not hearing the voice of God because it may be different than what we really want to hear.**

God truly has our best interest at heart and if He is telling us something, it is for our good, even if we can't see how at that moment. As Daughters of Freedom, it is imperative that we are able to heed the voice of God and the leading of the Holy Spirit. Allow me to share a few other examples from my own life.

In the chapter "False Positive," I talked about my last "official" relationship and briefly how I came to know he wasn't the one. For this chapter, I need to expound a bit on that situation as it relates to discerning the voice of God. As discussed, he appeared to be everything I knew I deserved – handsome, successful, Christian, and a gentleman. You've heard me say throughout the book how I am a believer in prophetic words and a few months before he and I met, I'd received a couple of different prophetic words from true men and women of God. When I met this guy, I just knew this was what the prophetic words they had spoken of concerned. While attending church with him one Sunday, his pastor called me to the front of the church and said to me, "You've had questions about something." He was absolutely right! Despite how great I thought the guy was and how great things were between us, something still didn't feel right. So the pastor was right, I did have questions about him. The pastor had the evangelist pray with me and one key thing I remember her saying was, "God has placed him in your life for a reason. He will be rooted like a tree and never leave you."

I was completely floored as she prayed directly about my question. I was certain then that this guy was the one and what I was experiencing were just my own insecurities since I couldn't remember a time I'd been treated so well. Not long after that, he started to become distant, eventually citing that I was not what he wanted. The situation devastated me because I felt I truly had heard from God about him being the one. The truth is, the unsettling feeling I was having was the Holy Spirit, but I trumped it up to insecurity. Because my self-worth was so low at that time, I felt that God could only speak to me through others, hence the prophetic words. I still believe the prophetic words spoken to me by the evangelist are true, but not for that guy. With her words to me, I believe God was trying to show me that her description of the guy for me did not line up with the current guy in my life. The reason I felt something wasn't right is because it wasn't. Anytime we receive prophetic words, it should be confirmed in our heart, and I never heard God tell me that particular guy was the one. Today, I look back on the evangelist's prayer and it became even clearer that the guy wasn't the one. Her words still ring in my ear: "He will be rooted like a tree and never leave." That guy was not rooted; he wanted to and did leave.

Another example I can share is in regards to the guy I dated who was incarcerated. Through most of my relationship with this guy I spent so much time asking God for sign after sign to confirm that is where I should be. I can remember one particular occasion where I visited him. It was probably the worst visit of our relationship and resulted in him leaving the visit after only 30 minutes. I was so upset as I drove back home that afternoon asking God once more for a sign that I was on the right track in staying in this relationship. When I was about 5 miles from my house, a police car from the city where the guy and I met passed me on the highway. Back then I wasn't able to effectively discern God's voice, and so my original thought was this was God's "reconfirmation" for me especially because the town we met in was four hours from where I currently lived. What were the odds that I'd see a cop car from where we met that far away, right when I was asking God for a sign? Today, as I've learned to discern the voice of God more effectively, I can say I misinterpreted that sign. I firmly still believe it was a message from God, but not confirming my staying in that situation—rather the opposite. Police cars can represent two things: someone who comes to save you from harm or someone who takes away something that isn't good. What God was saying to me through that cop car, with the name of where we met written on it right when I asked him for a sign was, "You've taken this situation too far and I'm trying to save you."

One last example I'd like to give doesn't relate to relationships but speaks to the evolvement of being able to discern the voice of God as you grow in relationship with Him. When I decided to go "public" with my story, my friend and I had a discussion regarding the platform that I'd use for my "coming out." Shortly after we got off of the phone, she called me back and told me she'd been asked to be part of a discussion group for CNN but was unable to, and perhaps it was something that could be good for me since we just talked about platforms. When she told me what the topic was about I felt uneasy because it wasn't one that I was well versed in. I think she could sense my hesitation and told me not to do it if I didn't feel comfortable with it. I spoke to the contact for the event, and we both agreed that I may not be the best fit. After we spoke, I prayed out loud, "God, if this is really for me, have him call me back." Well, sure enough, that morning the contact indeed called me back telling me he still needed more people. This should've seemed like an answered prayer, but there was still an uneasiness in my spirit. The event was in two hours so I didn't really have much time to decide. I couldn't discern if my uneasiness was a prompting from the Holy Spirit or if I was afraid of the opportunity. Then I remembered what I'd learn to do in crunch time situations. I'd go to my Bible and say, "Lord, please speak," and then just open it to a random passage. The passage that I opened to was about shame. How appropriate given the fact that one of my main focuses for women's ministry was overcoming shame. In that moment God was reminding me what my purpose platform was, and it wasn't the discussion that was going to be had at the CNN event.

You see, not being able to discern the voice of God can be detrimental because the enemy is crafty. He heard the conversation my friend and I had about platforms, and he delivered an opportunity that seemed perfect on the surface from a source the enemy knew I trusted, but the opportunity wasn't sent by God. Let me put a pin here and say that we need to vet all things through God, even things that come from people we know have our best interest at heart. That's just how crafty the enemy is. Even when I prayed the prayer asking God to have the contact call me back if the assignment was for me, the enemy heard that too. There is no telling what I would have been walked into had I taken that assignment. Yes, it was CNN, but remember the enemy seeks to kill, steal, and destroy. The enemy knows that God has called me to do a work and I could have gotten on that platform and said something that would haunt me later. That day, the Lord protected me and my future. This is why being able to discern the voice of God is so imperative.

I don't think we can effectively talk about discerning the voice God without talking about obedience. Not discerning the voice of God can lead to disobedience and for that there are consequences.

In one of my stories, I discussed how not heeding God's voice and deciding to do my own thing took me down a path where I almost lost everything. As discussed in the chapter "Rebound," my decision to move to another city for the guy was not God's will. In my disobedience and quest to do what I wanted to do, I took out a loan to move. Today, I have an unnecessary monthly payment that is a reminder of my disobedience. Could I pray and ask God to take the loan away so I'd have more financial freedom? Yes, but there are consequences to our disobedience. A good parent will not reward their child for disobedient acts. This is the same with our heavenly Father. We can't expect to do what we want and then ask Him to reward our disobedience or bless our mess. In my story, God granted me grace and mercy by opening doors for me to have some financial reprieve, but the loan payment still lingers as a reminder for me of the importance of obeying my heavenly Father from here forward.

# CHAPTER 24

# LEARNING TO TRUST GOD

*"Blessed is the man who trusts in the Lord, whose trust is the Lord. He is like a tree planted by water, that sendsout its roots by the stream, and does not fear when heat comes, for its leavs remain green, and is not anxious in the year of drought, for it does not cease to bear fruit"*
Jeremiah 17: 7-8 (NIV)

*"Trust in the Lord with all your heart and lean not on your own understanding."*
Proverbs 3:5 (NIV)

    One of the most beautiful places I've laid my eyes on is Corolla, NC. One day while my mother and I were on a beach trip, we decided we wanted to visit the local lighthouse. While there we saw a sign indicating that the pier would take us to the water. As we started to walk down the pier, I began to notice that it was built in the middle of a swampy area. If you know anything about me, you know that I am not a real wildlife person and the thought of coming up on a snake freaked me out. However, my mother really wanted to see it so we trucked on. As we walked farther and farther, the trees became denser, now starting to hover over us. At this point, I was too afraid to go any further and told my mother we had to turn around. We decided to walk to another portion of the park and ended up finding an alternate route to the sound. When I looked across the way I saw the pier that my mother and I had started walking on, realizing that right beyond the thicket that scared me was the water—I was so close.

This example reminds me of how life can be when we're trying to trust God. When we decide to live for Christ, our life journey becomes one where we walk by faith and not by sight. This can be very scary, especially if you suffer from control issues. When we walk by faith and not sight, it's as though we're walking hand in hand with God, but we are blindfolded, whereas He can see. In the example I used here, the location we were trying to get to was literally steps away, but fear of what was around me caused me to turn back.

Sometimes in life God desires to lead us to a place, but instead of keeping our eyes on Him, we focus on what seems scary around us so much so that we abort the mission even when the place He desires to lead us to is literally steps away. This always reminds me of the Scripture where Jesus beckoned Peter to walk to Him on the water. Peter truly did walk on water as long as he kept his eyes on Jesus, but the minute he turned his focus to the choppy sea around him, he began to sink. How far do you think Peter could have walked if he had kept his trust in God? Now ask yourself that same question? The beauty of this story is that my mother and I ended up finding the sound she wanted to see just through a much longer detour. This is the same for our lives. God will still get us to the place He was trying to lead us to even if our fears cause us to take detours that lengthen the destination.

I believe trusting God means exchanging our will for His. Growing up I often heard others say that God will give you the desires of your heart. As I am older, I now realize that is indeed true but only when we have fully submitted our lives to Him. When we do that, His will becomes our will, and His desires our desires. When we fully submit to God, we learn to lean not to our own understand trying to create our own life's directions, rather we follow God's directions for our life. I'm reminded of a funny story shared by my mother about cornbread. For years, she used Jiffy cornbread mix, which of course included step-by-step directions. One day she took it upon herself to get creative and alter the recipe by adding things like buttermilk and sugar. Well needless to say the cornbread was a disaster. Why? Because the mix didn't need any extra ingredients, and the recipe for the ingredients in the package was perfect. This is the same for life. God's Daughters of Freedom understand that He doesn't need our extra ingredients; following His directions always makes the recipe perfect.

# CHAPTER 25

# WAITING ON GOD

*"I would have fainted, unless I had believed to see the goodness of the Lord in the land of the living."*
Psalm 27:13

Wait, wait, wait, wait, wait. If you look up the definition for *wait*, you will likely see a picture of me. This is such a big topic, I need to take my time with this chapter. To be transparently honest, some days I do well at waiting and some days not so well. Some days I buy into the "patience is a virtue" concept, and some days I'm like bah humbug. Waiting can be very, *very* challenging, but also necessary. Scripture specifically talks about waiting on the Lord, and I'm a living witness that when I did not wait, rather taking matters into my own hands I have messed things up real, *real* good. As I sit writing this book as a single female with no prospects of seeing that change at the moment, I'm reminded once again that waiting is challenging.

When I was in high school my girlfriends and I would sit around after lunch and talk about what our future would be like. For me, I'd always state how I'd be married with at least one child by 28. Now you do the math—that plan seems to be a bit deferred. What I have learned in this life is that the best way to make God laugh is to tell Him what your plan is. One of my favorite Scriptures is *Jeremiah 29:11, "For I know the plans I have for you, said the Lord, plans to prosper and not harm you, plans to give you hope and a future"* (NIV). If you look closely at the Scripture, it doesn't talk about you and God developing a plan together, it says HE knows the plan HE has for you. The beauty is that He promises it to be a good plan so we can never go wrong with forgoing our plan and jumping onto God's wagon. Waiting can be hard in any aspect of life, but for the single woman, it will really stifle you if you allow it to. My preconceived notion for this comes from the fact that we live in a society that has put stipulations on what the standard should be for when a person should be married and start a family. I've had people make some very funny comments in my 20's around childbearing. For example, "Oh you're 25. Take my card. You don't want the batteries to run out on that clock, now do you?" Or, "You know a woman's peak egg production is at age 27; it's downhill from there." You have to love it, I tell you.

As a single woman in the wait, the issue is less about securing a mate and more about waiting for God to send you the one He has ordained for you. I've heard some contest the fact that God did not create one specific man for one specific woman, and that is their right to believe that, but I beg to differ. I believe in the biblical story of God removing a rib from Adam to make Eve, and that there is someone out here for me who is missing his rib, waiting for us to connect so he can get his rib back. At this place that God has brought me to in my life, I understand that marriage is not just about two people who love each other and decide they want to spend the rest of their lives together—it's ministry. It's to be an example to the world of how Christ loved the church. I believe God ordains people to be together for the uplifting of His kingdom—destiny partners. A part of the marriage ceremony says, "What God puts together…" The issue in today's time is that we are missing the most important piece, a marriage that is God-ordained.

When I think about my husband I think about a man who loves God, has a solid relationship with God, and understands we have work to do for the Kingdom. To sum it up in the words of a wonderful friend, "I need a man who can help usher me into the Holy Spirit." Yes and amen! Ladies, if you are a Christian woman, please do not do as I've done on many occasions and think it's okay to connect with a man who is a non-believer or is a lukewarm believer. You want a man who can be the spiritual leader of your household, and if his Bible is collecting dust, well you know the rest. God's Daughters of Freedom are not on a quest to "get 'em and change 'em." The man of God for you should know who he is in the Lord before you even meet.

When we are in the season of waiting for our mate, we can also fall into the trap of making our sole focus being in the wait. When our sole focus is on being in the wait, many times we can't allow ourselves to even go anywhere without having the thought, "Ooh let me go, because I might meet my husband there." For me, I couldn't go anywhere just to enjoy myself. It was always because I didn't want to miss the chance of meeting "the one." For the Christian woman, it gets even hazier because we attempt to manipulate God by staking claim on a man we have a crush on and convince ourselves that God said he was "the one." The only thing is sister so and so also said she heard the same thing, and that doesn't add up. Remember God is not the author of confusion. I could be wrong, but I believe if you want to know if God is, in fact, saying that man is the one for you, wait to see if he actually approaches you. I believe God would give him that same sentiment about you if it were so.

When I began to reflect on past situations in my life, where I didn't wait on the Lord, especially those that dealt with my relationships with men, the word *sacrifice* kept coming to mind. As I perused Merriam-Webster's various definitions of *sacrifice* the one that stood out to me stated, "A destruction or surrender of something for the sake of something else"[5]. Both the words "destruction" and "surrender" seem so weighty but appropriate at the same time. For years, I spent my life "destroying" and "surrendering" myself for all the men, except the One I should have been sacrificing for, and the One who gave the ultimate sacrifice for me – my heavenly Father. When we are broken inside, we will give up everything to feel fixed only to later realize our sacrifices left us feeling more broken. This is why it is so important to wait on the Lord.

As I'm in the season of waiting I have found great comfort in a poem by the spoken word poet Janette McGhee. The poem is entitled, *I Will Wait for You*. It rocked me to my core from the first moment I heard it. She tells this story of how instead of waiting for God, we get involved in these relationships or situationships that we think we can manipulate into being God-ordained, but it never works out. But then she makes up in her mind that she was going to stop doing things her way and truly wait on God, even being content with just Him if He called her to a life of singleness. That last part is a place that I feel truly comes with real growth in Christ.

We as women crave relationship and God loves relationship, but He does not want any relationship over the one we have with Him—He is a jealous God. I truly believe that before God will release

---

[5]  Merriam-Webster. Accessed February 28, 2016. http://www.merriam-webster.com/dictionary/sacrifice.

the man He has for us, He has to know that He can trust us not to ditch our relationship with Him when He sends our mate. Let's be clear here, we cannot fool God. On many occasions I've told the Lord, "Okay God, You and I are tighter than ever, no man will ever take your place," and as soon as one showed me any type of real attention I was ready to throw caution to the wind. God also knows the level of our healing.

> *Before God will release the man He has for us, He has to know that He can trust us not to ditch our relationship with Him when He sends our mate.*

Up until this point in my life, I have been such a broken mess that I honestly would not have been able to fully receive the man God had for me without messing it up real good. He knew this because He knows me. So today, my prayer is less of, "God, please send me my husband," and more of, "God, thank you for my future husband, and please help prepare me to be a wife." Many of us want the husband totally forgetting that we have an important role to play as well—helpmate, and sometimes this requires preparation. If you want an example of what characteristics a wife or helpmate should portray, consider reading Proverbs 31. This Scriptural text is often referred to as the text on the "virtuous woman." Daughters of Freedom should strive to wear this title. If you want to do something else while you're waiting on your man of God, cover him in prayer, praying that God would continue to breathe a fresh anointing in his life, and prepare him to be a husband.

    I'd be remiss if I wrote this portion of the book and acted like I didn't have days where I wondered if God had forgotten me. One of my key focuses in life is releasing my will for God's will, and I told the Lord that if He didn't see fit for me to marry, I would be okay with just Him, and I'd ask that He remove my desire for marriage.

I'm a believer that God loves us too much to see us in turmoil, and if marriage wasn't in my future why would He still allow me to desire something greatly that He knew was never in His plan for my life? If I can be transparently honest, I've had moments where I'd go to God and ask Him for a reminder that He hadn't forgotten about me. One particular time when I prayed this prayer, the following day I went to the mail and there was a mailer from Best Buy that said, "Congratulations on your engagement. Here is a coupon for $25 off when you sign up for Best Buy's Wedding Registry." I was so tickled by this because it didn't make sense that Best Buy would send me anything about getting engaged. Some may consider that coincidence, but I consider it a little note from God saying, "I haven't forgotten you."

While waiting for God to send our destiny partner, there is another struggle that the single Christian woman faces. Sexual desires. This is a "keep it real" book, so let me keep doing that. Because we are fleshly beings, whether married or not, we have sexual desires. The issue is that when we are not married, we are not to act on those desires because according to Scripture fornication is a sin, and we know sin is not pleasing to God. As I'm sure you're aware of from my story, I've called myself a Christian a lot longer than the time I've been actually practicing celibacy. Notice that I said I called myself a Christian. My behavior was most certainly not Christ-like when I knowingly let men who were not my husband fall in and out of my bed.

At this place in my life, I'm fully aware of my humanistic desires, but I'm determined to let my desire to please God override the desire to temporarily please my flesh. When taking a vow of celibacy, you should be fully prepared for attacks from the enemy to try and get you to falter. I can recall meeting what I thought was a nice gentleman who appeared to be everything on paper, but early on I began noticing our conversations starting to have sexual undertones with his sending me random picture messages of scantily covered body parts. A lot of his conversation was around various sexual fantasies that he wanted me to partake in. To be completely transparent, I would participate in these discussions but that was not right and the Holy Spirit convicted me.

I chose to listen to the promptings of the Holy Spirit and tell him I was celibate. His response to me was I should have said that in the beginning so as to not have wasted his time. I was certainly appalled by this but thought it was the end. Perhaps, in the beginning, he should have said all he was interested in was sex. I thought my celibacy announcement would run him away, but it made him come on stronger. The situation truly had me baffled because I knew he could have any woman he wanted, and likely one who was willing to sleep with him, so why was he bothering with me? One day I asked God to show me what this was all about. Immediately after that prayer, I closed my eyes and saw a big snake staring back at me. This guy was a trap set by the enemy. I'll touch on this a bit more in a later chapter, but we need to be mindful that the enemy is not prancing around here in a red suit with horns and a pitchfork. He can come in a package that we think we want and we think is good for us, but we must pray for discernment.

Like many times before, I could have given into this guy in the hopes that it would've turned into a relationship, but that was no longer who I was, and the relationship I was most concerned with was the one with my Heavenly Father. According to this guy, this was a day and age where sex was a "huge part of adult relationships" and I was never going to find a man who wanted to "buy the car without taking it for a test drive." We are indeed living in a time where premarital sex is the rule and not the exception. I have to also be honest and say that I was a bit worried about his comment wondering would my "radicalness" keep me from finding a husband. Here I was already in my thirties with no prospects. But I'm reminded of *Romans 12:1*, *"Therefore, I urge you, brothers and sisters, in view of God's mercy, to offer your bodies as a living sacrifice, holy and pleasing to God—this is your true and proper worship"* (NIV).

When we present a sacrifice to God it is to be of the best quality. Our bodies are no exception. We can't in good conscious provide our bodies as a living sacrifice to God when we're filled with sexual impurity, allowing men who are not our husbands to invade the place where the Holy Spirit resides. You would also think finding a godly man who shared the same views as you on celibacy wouldn't be a challenge, but I'm here to tell you, that is not always the case. What I've found with Christian men I've encountered is that they are in an even greater struggle and sometimes want to play around with the notion of, "how much can we do, and still be saved."

Sex should never be used as a bargaining tool, nor does it keep a person around. If a person truly loves you, they will do so whether you are offering sex of any kind or not. The whole, "if you love me, then you will do it" is played out. During a period of celibacy later in life, I quickly learned how my "no sex" policy became a wonderful weeding out tool for the Mr. Wrongs. During my walk with Christ, sex has been one of those areas where I've really had to allow Him to work on me, especially because it was what I used to try and make men love me. The healthier I became and the more I grew in Christ, the more I learned what was important. At the end of the day, I choose to not compromise. I choose to be obedient to that which my Father (God) requires of me. I choose to trust that He knows the desires of my heart and will reward me in due season.

Let me get really honest here and tell you that if this is a problem area in your life, you must consistently and continually ask

God to strengthen you until you are unwavering. As said before, we are in the world but not of the world. We are human and have human desires which mean we are not immune to temptation. The question becomes how do we fight this temptation and stay obedient to God? To answer this question I'm reminded of *James 4:7-8,* *"Submit yourselves, then, to God. Resist the devil, and he will flee from you. Come near to God and he will come near to you"* (NIV). What this Scripture means to me is that you must be diligent in resisting temptation, and seeking God's face and His Word to help you stay strong.

We need to realize that temptation can come in a variety of ways, some we don't even think about like music or television. Growing up in my household, my mother was a true stickler for the types of music or television shows that were allowed to be played in our home. I can remember my friend allowing me to borrow a movie and we came home one day after school to watch it but couldn't find it anywhere. I called my mom at work and asked her what happened to the movie. Her response to me was, "I put it on the grill. I'm not having those spirits coming into our house." At the time I thought it was funny yet crazy that my mother would put the DVD on the actual cooking grill, but today I realize her seriousness about protecting what went into her family's spirit.

This is the same for when you are single and trying not to fall in the pit of fornication. When trying to fight temptation of the flesh, you cannot go around listening to music that talks about being flipped up and rubbed down all night long or watch television or movies with scenes that promote sexual activity. These things may seem subliminal, but remember the devil is the prince of the air and he will use anything to knock you off your game. One minute you're watching a "harmless" movie and the next minute your thoughts turn to things that aren't Christ-like. Those are not coincidences, those are traps from the enemy hoping to make you fall. Sometimes as single Christian women we can be solid on waiting to have sex until marriage but still desiring to deal with our sexual desires until God sends our destiny partner. Therein comes the conversation around masturbation, or the act of pleasing oneself. Remaining transparent, I have to be honest and say masturbation was something I struggled with. There is much controversy about whether Scripture specifically speaks about masturbation being a sin, but I do know that Scripture speaks about lust being a sin. This may not be impossible, but it would appear that it is difficult to self-please without lusting. In the case of masturbation, lusting would be having sexual fantasies that you think of while pleasing yourself. Again, because Scripture doesn't speak about masturbation specifically, I'd say allow the Holy Spirit to guide you. One thing I love about the Holy Spirit is that if He is truly living on the inside of you, there will be a level of conviction that tells you whether your behavior is pleasing to God or not.

When we are in a season of waiting, we can sometimes get caught in the comparison trap and become distracted from moving forward in our own lanes by focusing on the lane of another. This is a real tactic of the enemy especially when it concerns areas of our life where we feel we are in lack. In my life, God has blessed me abundantly professionally, but I never desired to be one of those women who was married to their careers. My thought process has always been God first, family, then career, yet it seemed the second most important thing was lacking. I saw my friends and family find love and start families, while it appeared the only love I had was my career. I had to begin limiting my social media intake because everywhere I looked it appeared a friend was getting engaged, married, or having a baby.

There was never the issue of me not being happy for my friends because it was wonderful that God was blessing them.

However, I did feel a bit of sadness for me, not understanding why God wasn't doing the same in my life. If we are not careful, the enemy will cause us to focus so much on the lives of others that we take on a coveting spirit, and that is not of God. When we begin to focus on the lives of others we stop focusing on our own paths. We absolutely have to remember that God gave each of us a path and a lane to swim in. The enemy has no desire to see us flourish in the lane God gave us to swim, so he will turn our focus over to someone else's lane. We can't swim straight ahead while focusing on someone else's lane. What I have found solace in is the fact that everything God has for me is for me. Just because I don't reach a certain swim marker that another may have already, does not mean God doesn't have that marker for me somewhere else down my lane. In a sermon a while back I heard a preacher say, "If God is blessing those around you, don't be jealous. Be grateful because it means He is on your pew."

In our lives, waiting doesn't have to just be around love and relationships. We wait for lots of things including areas of our professional career. When I worked at my last corporate job, I enjoyed the work but management was a challenge. In addition to that, I was coming into the place in my life where God was showing me my purpose and it didn't line up with the 9-5 corporate America atmosphere, so I began growing restless. I was trying to figure out how to get in a position where I could focus on my "purpose projects" while also having enough finances to sustain my livelihood. I began asking God, "Am I supposed to quit and just jump? I have financial responsibilities and can't be without a secure income. Do you want me to move back home?" I wasn't hearing Him say anything, which for me equated to "wait." I began seeking other full-time jobs mainly because I was ready to move on, but I was not even getting interviews for those I knew I was qualified for. I simply could not understand this, but I knew God was still saying, "Wait."

About 6 months later, a friend sent me a job description for a position that sounded exactly like what I was doing, so I wasn't completely sure I wanted the job. I ended up applying and learned that the position was being offered as an independent contractor, essentially requiring only part-time hours that I could set for myself. Goodbye to my restrictive 9-5 Corporate America job. I felt as though God was saying, "Here you go. The last two years have prepared you for this assignment. Your finances will be taken care of, and you'll have the time to work on the 'purpose projects.' Anything else?" The icing on the cake confirming how I know my God is always in control was hearing these words from the hiring manager for the contractor job, "We hadn't even planned to create this position." Here I'm reminded of *Isaiah 43:19*, *"Behold, I will do a new thing; now it shall spring forth; shall you not know it? I will even make a way in the wilderness, and rivers in the desert."* As I type right now, I am sitting in my home office, on a day that I was able to set aside just for writing thanks to my new flexible schedule. Wait, I say on the Lord!

As I close this chapter, allow me to reiterate that waiting can come with its challenges. I believe it's *how* we wait that will prove whether we succeed or fail. Just the other day the enemy attacked my mind as soon as I walked in the door about being alone. I started to feel sorry for myself, which is what the enemy wanted. I went into my prayer closet and laid before the Lord. Why? Because He knows the path I take. While we are in the wait, we have to learn to wait not just *on* God, but *in* God. Waiting in God means that when the enemy attacks, we run to God for shelter. That is the only way we will truly find the peace that surpasses all understanding while we wait. Sometimes we may even wonder if waiting is worth it, but I'm reminded of *Galatians 6:9*, *"And let us not grow weary of doing good, for in due season we will reap, if we do not give up."* (NIV) God has not forgotten about you or me.

CHAPTER 26

# THIS IS WAR: REALIZING WHO THE REAL ENEMY IS

I know the enemy hates me, and I hate him equally so. So much that I didn't even want to devote an entire chapter to talking about him, but I feel as Daughters of Freedom we may underestimate the enemy and his desire to see nothing good come of us. As a child, whenever I'd see an image of the devil he was depicted as this character wearing a fire red jumpsuit with a long tail and horn carrying a pitchfork. As an adult, I am fully cognizant that depiction of the devil is completely false. The enemy is walking around in a form just like you and me, and he is slicker than the finest baby oil. What I feel to be the greatest movie of all time was released in 2015. It's entitled, *War Room*. Seeing that movie truly changed my life. The premise for the movie is about understanding who our real enemy is and identifying the best strategy to fight him in war. In *John 10:10* Scripture says, *"The thief cometh not, but for to steal, and to kill, and to destroy: I am come that they might have life, and that they might*

*have it more abundantly."* In my life, he has tried to use my past to steal, kill, and destroy me. Up until this point, he's had a good run at it, but the table is now turning. Sharing my story is a direct reversal of his tactic against me.

What I love about the movie *War Room* is that it gives a clear example of the fact that the way we should be fighting the enemy is in prayer and time spent with God. When we stop acting in our own strength and allow God to fight our battles, we begin experiencing what the scripture speaks about in Exodus 14:13 and 2 Chronicles 20:17—we get to stand still and watch God give us the victory! Think back to the situation I mentioned in the last chapter where it concerned my career. In that situation, the enemy was really trying to steal my joy, and he was winning until I realized I was fighting the battle the wrong way. The enemy had me wound so tight I became bitter and began suffering from anxiety attacks. The enemy wanted me to focus on my circumstance and not what God said in His Word. God wanted me to be patient, content, and trusting. Fighting the enemy God's way keeps us in perfect peace while fighting our own way will keep us in turmoil.

The movie *War Room* focuses on an actual physical space being set aside just for prayer and time spent with God. Yes, it's true that we can pray to God anywhere, any time of the day, but there is something special about a designated place just for fellowship with God.

> ***Fighting the enemy God's way keeps us in perfect peace while fighting our own way will keep us in turmoil.***

In fact *Matthew 6:6 says, "But when you pray, go into your room, close the door and pray to your Father, who is unseen. Then your*

*Father, who sees what is done in secret, will reward you"* (NIV). I was so smitten by this verse and the movie that I decided to create my own war room. My apartment only had one walk-in closet, and my dilemma was what I would do with my clothes if I used it for my war room. I had to decide what was more important to me, having space with a door that hides the fact that I likely have too much stuff, or having a secret space where I can go to be clothed in things not material. I chose the latter and became creative with how to store my clothes—storage organizers and rolling racks in the corner of my bedroom. It has been functional, and also forces me to keep my clothes more organized since they are now in plain view—sounds like a win-win. My war room has changed my prayer life, and I now know how to fight the enemy the right way.

On so many occasions the enemy has tried to play me, but I wasn't fully aware that it was his work. Today I know his m.o. and he isn't coming with any new tricks. Be mindful that the enemy knows your weaknesses and those are often the areas where he will try to attack you the hardest. Even Jesus was tempted by satan in the wilderness, but He used the Word of God to cause him to flee. We must be the same way. As Daughters of Freedom, it's imperative that we know God's Word, so that we have something to throw at the devil when he comes, and he will come again and again.

Don't forget the enemy is not prancing around in a red suit; he will use people to try and get to you. For example, perhaps you have a supervisor who is just very nasty to you or even a loved one who attacks your character. Remember Scripture says in *Ephesians 6:12, "For we wrestle not against flesh and blood, but against principalities, against powers, against the rulers of the darkness of this world, against spiritual wickedness in high places."* This means that for those people who seem to get under your skin or mistreat you for no reason, it's rarely about them, but about the enemy using them to get to you. And the enemy will use ANYBODY; he doesn't care.

    We should also be mindful that one of the greatest tactics of the enemy is to attack our mind. In my opinion, that can be worse than his using a person to get to us. It's in our mind where he can plant seeds of deception and stir up all types of confusion. In my life, he has used my low self-worth to create stories in my head about things that weren't true at all. For example, if I sent someone an email or a text message and they didn't respond in a timely fashion, the enemy would have me make up stories wondering if I said something wrong, or if they were mad at me, or how rude of them, or any crazy idea that wasn't necessarily true. The truth was that more often than not, the person either couldn't respond at the moment or simply forgot to respond, but it was nothing about what I thought. The enemy will use any opportunity he can to steal your peace. You see he knows that peace is what keeps us sane even when everything else around us seems to be crumbling. If he can rob us of that, he will think he won.

    As I close this chapter out, allow me to tell you that I'm no longer afraid of the enemy. When speaking of the enemy the reference is often made to the snake. All of my life I have been extremely afraid of snakes and would still be taken aback if I walked up on one unknowingly. My fear was so bad that I couldn't even see a snake in a book, on television, or even places like the aquarium. This year, as I've learned more about who my real enemy is I've been committed to taking a firm stand against him and his lies. When I visited the aquarium earlier this year, I conquered one of my greatest fears. I walked right up to the tank with the snakes and looked directly at them. This was my metaphorical notice to satan that I will not be running from him anymore. As Daughters of Freedom, we should be ever reminded that God will never allow the enemy to go but so far, so there is no need to fear him. Allow me to offer you a suggestion for a good read for women who want to gain more awareness of how the enemy attacks. Priscilla Shirer recently published a book entitled, *Fervent*. The book focuses solely on specific areas where satan attacks women. Allow me to go on the record as saying, it will change your life for the better!

CHAPTER 27

# LET FREEDOM RING

I think it only befitting to close the book out talking about FREEDOM! One of my favorite passages in Scripture is when Jesus raised Lazarus from the dead. Scripture tells us that Mary and Martha sent word to Jesus that their brother Lazarus was very sick, but Jesus didn't come immediately. In fact, by the time Jesus arrived, Lazarus had been dead for four days. Death was no match for the King of Kings, and Scripture tells us that Jesus raised Lazarus. For many years of my life, I've been in bondage and dead on the inside seeking all the wrong things to bring me back to life, when the only one who truly had the resurrection power was the King of Kings, my Heavenly Father.

One of the "lie limbs" from the enemy's tree in my life was that there was no way I could start sharing my story without having a mate as evidence that someone thought I was worthy in spite of my past. It was in one of my tear-drenched moments where I laid prostrate at the feet of God that He spoke to me and said, "Samantha, you are what honor points to." This revelation almost knocked me off of my feet. I was the evidence. I was the living proof of who God is and what He could do! I'm the evidence of someone being lost and found, broken and restored, freed from chains of bondage. I should've been dead, but God! I am that which honor points to. So know that today, when you see me, you see victory! The tree that grew from the seed the enemy planted in my life long ago has been uprooted, and I've given him the firewood to take back to hell with him!

When I think about what going from a life of bondage to freedom looks like, I think about the story of Jesus turning the water into wine at the wedding. *John 2:9-10, says "and the master of the banquet tasted the water that had been turned into wine. He did not realize where it had come from, though the servants who had drawn the water knew. Then he called the bridegroom aside and said, 'Everyone brings out the choice wine first and then the cheaper wine after the guests have had too much to drink; but you have saved the best till now.'"*

What the enemy meant for bad, God has made good, and He has saved the best for last! My latter shall be greater than my past! I read something somewhere that said, "The only reason you should ever look back is to see how far you've come." I believe this is true to an extent. I don't believe we should spend our lives living in the past, but I also think it is important to look back to remember our testimony and to help our sisters get free.

I pray that sharing my journey from bondage to freedom with you has given you a living testament that God is the only one who can set you free, and wants to see you free! I thank God for giving me beauty for ashes, the oil of joy for my mourning, and the garment of praise for the spirit of heaviness (see Isaiah 61:3). Many are the afflictions of the righteous, but God truly does deliver them from them all (see Psalm 34:19). Growing up the church choir would often sing the song by Rev. Milton Brunson, entitled *I'm Free*. The chorus to that song says,

> I'm Free
> Praise the Lord, I'm free
> No longer bound
> No more chains holding me
> My soul is resting
> It's just a blessing
> Praise the Lord
> Hallelujah, I'm free

I now consider that song my anthem because God has indeed set me free from a life of bondage to the lies of the enemy. Praise the Lord, I'm free! Won't you join me?

# About the Author

Samantha Overton is a woman on a mission, a Christ-driven mission that is. After spending many years in Corporate America, she began experiencing symptoms of restlessness, believing that God had another plan for her life greater than the one she had. Little did she know that God's plan would involve a part of her of life she never thought she'd have the courage to share. There Samantha realized God had a place for her in women's ministry. Samantha's quest in life now is to use her own life's journey to help other women move from bondage to freedom, living out the life that God purposed for them.

To contact the author for speaking engagements, conferences, book tours and signings, write

**Visit www.fallenchains.com**
**E-mail: info@samanthaoverton.com**

## Other Authors by
## COOKE PUBLISHING HOUSE

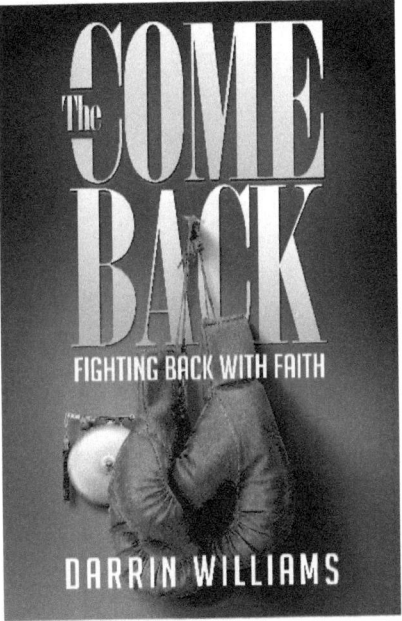

The Comeback chronicles the life of Pastor Darrin Williams, as told through snapshots of his life from boyhood to the present. It is a story of redemption and reformation as Darrin undergoes a complete 180 degree turn from the life of a gangbanger and drug dealer to one who fully established his belief and trust in God. He took the unlikeliest of life's circumstances and became a firm believer in God, showing that all things are possible to those who believe.
**ISBN: 978-0-9979923-2-8**

For more information, visit
www.fightwithmyfaith.com

# Other Authors by
# COOKE PUBLISHING HOUSE

Sometimes getting up early doesn't always have to be a chore; it can sometimes be a delightful adventure that will shape and change your life forever. Walk with Rolinda Butler in Early Morning Visitor as she navigates you through a journey of spiritual discovery and a closer relationship with the Holy Spirit.

ISBN: 978-0-9979923-0-4

For more information, visit
www.earlymorningvisitor.com

## Other Authors by
## COOKE PUBLISHING HOUSE

The Love Between challenges you to let go of your past and walk into the light and love of Jesus Christ. Author Tiffany Hayes shares many of her personal stories in an effort to spread the message that God loves you no matter what you have done, said, or been. Tiffany discusses topics such as pride, rejection, and low self-esteem that may cause you to question the love between you and God. Ultimately, she bridges the gap so you are able to fully embrace God's love and share it with others.
**ISBN: 978-0-9979923-4-2**

For more information, visit
www.thelovebetween.com

www.ingramcontent.com/pod-product-compliance
Lightning Source LLC
Chambersburg PA
CBHW021126300426
44113CB00006B/306